John Dyson

The Motorcycling Book

Illustrated by Lionel Willis

Kestrel Books

131) KAWASAKI - Z 400

KESTREL BOOKS
Published by Penguin Books Ltd,
Harmondsworth, Middlesex, England

Copyright © 1977 by John Dyson
Illustrations Copyright © 1977 by Lionel Willis

Published in hardback by Kestrel Books, 1977
Reprinted 1977, 1979
Published simultaneously in paperback by Peacock Books

ISBN 0 7226 5293 3

Printed in Great Britain by
Fletcher & Son Ltd, Norwich

27) BULTACO - CHISPA

Contents

Acknowledgements

The author acknowledges with grateful thanks
the help and interest of the following individuals
and organizations:

The Metropolitan Police Driving School, London
Heron Suzuki GB Ltd
Sgt Colin Gooding (Automobile Association)
Auto-Cycle Union
Michael Evans
Castrol
Shell
Horsham Schoolboy Scramble Club
Nick Jeffery
Nick Barnes
The librarian, Royal Automobile Club
British Motorcyclists' Federation

Introduction

On the question of motorcycle safety there are two widely differing views. Enthusiasts know that motorcycles are convenient, reasonably cheap, and lots of fun; others know that motorcycles can also be dangerous. This book is intended to bridge that gap. It introduces readers to the pleasures, costs, and responsibilities of motorcycling. It also helps them to understand the risks and the problems.

Even for young people with no driving experience there is no doubt that the risks can be reduced to an acceptable level. This means that riders must know the risks, and be able to recognize – and avoid – them on the road.

Safe motorcycling begins with the choice of a suitable machine for the age and level of experience of the rider. It includes knowledge of how the machine works, and how to maintain it. On the road it requires skill, decisiveness, and a defensive attitude of mind – 'When that driver makes a mistake *I* won't be in the way.'

The information on safe riding in this book has been provided by instructors at the Metropolitan Police Driving School. They are the country's acknowledged experts, with lifetimes of experience in the saddle. Inexperienced motorcyclists will learn much from their rational approach.

The book does not cover driving rules, which are contained in the Highway Code. Nor does it include the kind of detailed maintenance instructions that are found in the owner's handbook provided with every new machine. Both these books are essential reading.

I Your first motorcycle

1 The joy of two-wheelers

It is not difficult for anybody over the age of sixteen to buy and ride a moped or motorcycle. The cost is within easy reach of most young people who work or do school-holiday jobs. What you buy is not merely a machine with two wheels, but a wonderful sense of freedom and independence that can hardly be imagined by those content to wait at bus stops or sit in cars.

A motorcycle is a magic carpet because it takes you where you want to go at little cost. It saves time and provides freedom. And it is a passport because it enables you to do new things and go to new places. In this sense the advantages of cheap and convenient personal transport can help you to achieve an aim or to broaden your life.

There are many different types of motorcycles. The different sizes are graded by engine capacity, which is measured in cubic centimetres (cc). If the 50cc moped is the Mini of the bike world, the 125cc motorcycle is an Escort or Allegro, the 250cc is comparable with a Cortina, and the larger 500cc or 750cc machines are Rovers and Triumphs. Then there are the 'superbikes' equivalent to Jaguars and Ferraris, and the trail bikes, made for driving on roads and going cross-country, which are perhaps comparable to souped-up Land Rovers.

The large machines can cost as much as a small car. To handle them you must be an enthusiast and an expert, so for obvious reasons this book concerns mainly the smaller and cheaper kind of machine that young people can more easily afford.

A new motorcycle of about 125cc is big enough to be comfortable and handle reasonably well, and it has sufficient power to carry a pillion passenger and keep up with traffic in towns. This type of machine is ideal for commuting. Compared with a secondhand family saloon car in reasonable condition it is less than a quarter of the cost to purchase and to run. A two-wheeler with a modest engine goes four or five times farther on a gallon of petrol. It dabbles through traffic jams as if they did not exist. Parking is always easy and is usually free. And in the last resort a motorcycle is easier to push.

But a motorcycle is more than just a means to an end. It is also enjoyable in its own right. You don't have to ride a glamorous and high-powered machine to experience the pleasure of cruising the open road – the press of warm wind in your face, the tarmac uncoiling beneath your front wheel as you lean the machine into bends with the rhythm of a downhill skier . . .

Riding a motorbike you feel different. You are more of a pioneer, an adventurer. Travelling from one place to another is not a chore but fun. In a car you are insulated from the smell and feeling of the countryside. Sitting out in the wind on a motorcycle, you might be spitting midges from between your teeth but you feel a sense of accomplishment and adventure – a real knight of the road.

Unhappily there are disadvantages. A motorcycle is not in the least glamorous or exciting in rain, fog, or freezing weather. Nor is there much that is pleasant (apart from the satisfaction of being able to jump the queue) in filtering through the exhaust smoke of lines of cars and lorries.

A motorcyclist *must* wear a crash helmet, and should wear strong gloves, boots, and a protective suit. It can take five minutes to 'tog up' before driving away, and nearly as long to undress when you stop. It is difficult to wear a natty suit underneath a motorcycling outfit and it might not always convey the best impression to walk into an appointment or an interview swinging a briefcase in one hand and a crash helmet in the other.

As a piece of machinery a motorcycle is simple and satisfying to operate. But it is extremely difficult to control *well*. Only an experienced rider knows that any fool can ride fast, and that it takes a real expert to stop. This is not a question merely of applying the brakes in a way that avoids a skid. It is a matter of knowing *when* to slow down or stop to avoid an accident before it happens.

In a car you are protected by seatbelts and a steel shell from the mistakes and stupidities of your own and other people's driving. On a motorcycle your only protection is awareness and quick thinking. That protection is sufficient, but only for as long as you keep it up. When vigilance falters, accidents happen. So everything is up to you – the rider.

2   The story of motorcycles

The first motorcycle really was a hot piece of machinery. It was powered by steam, with a boiler under the saddle and a steam-pressure gauge mounted on the handlebars. Every mile or so the rider had to dismount and stoke the boiler, and no doubt relieve the heat in the seat of his pants. The time was the middle of last century, when new railway lines were being built at a furious rate, and inventors were trying to put locomotive power on two wheels.

These early machines were invented in France and called motor-velocipedes, but very little is known about them. They must have been most uncomfortable and difficult to ride, and none was notably successful. Some were built as tricycles, and these three-wheelers served as test-beds for different kinds of engines then being invented.

In fact the very first practical petrol engine was fitted not to a car but to a two-wheeler. Designed and patented in 1885 by Dr N. A. Otto and Gottlieb Daimler, and successfully ridden the following year, it looked more like a two-wheeled threshing machine than a motorcycle.

While Daimler went on to build the first 'horseless carriage' from what was really a four-wheeled motorcycle, other designers produced a weird assortment of machinery to push along the standard bicycle. Engines were built into the wheel, mounted on handlebars, put under the seat and even built on outriggers that stuck out behind rather like the outboard engine of a boat.

In those days, at the end of last century, roads were dusty, pot-holed, and strewn with flints and horseshoe nails. Punctures happened frequently and had to be fixed at the road-side. Petrol was cheap but difficult to get, because there were no service stations as we know them today.

Severe bumping upset the machinery, which needed constant adjustment. Riding was painful because there were no springs. Starting the engine required luck, magic, and a prayer. There was no clutch, no gears, and the engine was very inflexible, so once it started (with luck) you had to get aboard quickly. When it was necessary to stop on the road, perhaps to let a traction engine go by, the motor also stopped. But in that age when horsepower was fuelled by oats and hay you can imagine how exciting it must have been to ride independently through the countryside raising clouds of smoke and dust and making a kind of popping, roaring noise like that of a dumper truck.

By the turn of the century engines were mounted low, near the pedals, so the machines were more stable. You still had to pedal for dear life to get up a hill, and on the flat it was difficult to beat an ordinary bicycle. You had to remember to pump oil into the cylinder every few minutes. There was always a spare leather drive-belt coiled up and tied beneath the saddle.

In Britain the speed limit for motor vehicles was twenty miles an hour and if you went too fast policemen hiding behind hedges with stopwatches were liable to spring out and flag you down. For this reason motor racing first started abroad, in 1895, with the inter-city car and motorcycle racing marathons between European capitals such as Paris and Vienna, or Paris and Madrid. As many as three million spectators lined the routes and many were killed by cars running out of control. In 1904 international motorcycle racing started on a speedway-type track made entirely of wooden boards. There was also a kind of drag racing: at a meeting in 1903 the winning machine covered the mile from a standing start in seventy-six seconds (the current British record is twenty-six seconds).

Many improvements were made to motorcycles during the decade prior to the First World War. Tyres became bigger and better. Spring suspension made riding less of a bone-jarring experience. Speedometers and other instruments were fitted. Kick-starters were introduced so you no longer had to push the machine along, running, then leap into the saddle when the engine fired. Improved controls made handling easier. The rear wheel was driven by chain instead of the leather belt which tended to slip in wet weather.

As roads became better and smoother, motorcycles were fitted with sidecars, often made of wicker. Motorcycles now were being considered as a means of transport, but up to the 1920s the top speed of a typical $3\frac{1}{2}$ horsepower touring machine was only about 40 mph.

After the First World War people were generally more mechanically minded. While motorcycling almost died in America because so many cheap cars were made available, in Britain it became very popular: in 1922 there were 245,000 cars but 370,000 motorcycles. Some of the technology developed to build fighter planes was adapted for motorcycles, and there were more than 100 firms offering more than 200 types of machine for sale. Some were peculiar, like the first motor scooters – low-wheeled platforms pushed by tiny engines and ridden in a standing position.

By the 1930s Britain led the world in motorcycle design and engineering. In world competition British riders and machines were top of the tree. Events like the famous Isle of Man TT (Tourist Trophy) Race, which had been started in 1907 to avoid the speed limit problem, were supreme tests in which British riders and machines excelled. Engines were now very powerful, but not until 1936 was the suspension of motorcycles good enough to keep both wheels on the ground after hitting a modest bump.

Competition became increasingly tough and by the Second World War British machines began to lose their lead in the sport to challenges from BMW from Germany and Gilera from Italy. With refinements like telescopic front forks and coil ignition, motorcycles became more reliable and more comfortable. Famous British names like Velocette, AJS, Matchless, BSA, Norton, and Triumph were still in great demand. They were big, beefy, well-behaved machines. By the 1950s there were also many British firms making small motorcycles, mostly using the same small Villiers engine, and the only challenge came from Vespa and Lambretta motor scooters.

These were the first machines to be built for those who wanted transport and nothing else, and were the first machines to benefit from the huge teenager market. The engine was enclosed because it was reliable enough not to require constant attention. They had an open frame with a flat footboard, so riders could wear town clothes and keep reasonably dry and clean. They were a brand-new product that answered the post-war demand for cheap transport. And they swept the world.

Meanwhile, however, a Japanese engineer had developed a new engine. During the Second World War it had run on a fuel made from the roots of pine trees. In 1948 the engineer began manufacturing motorcycles. By 1962 one million machines had been made and in international competition the name was world famous. That year a little over 4,000 machines were imported by Britain. The following year 50,000 were imported; in 1964 that number doubled. The name was Honda.

Under such a furious assault practically all the small British manufacturers making small motorcycles closed down. Their machines were unreliable and unsophisticated compared with the Japanese Honda which came ready-equipped with such refinements as traffic indicators, mirrors, and electric starter. The big British motorcycles such as Triumphs and Nortons continued in production, but apart from police forces and a few enthusiasts not many people wanted them. It was not until about 1970 that Japanese manufacturers turned out bigger machines. The few surviving British firms immediately struck serious financial difficulty and by 1976 the number of British motorcycles being produced every year numbered only a few score.

The market boomed. In 1975 more than 250,000 motorcycles were sold in Britain, 60 per cent of them to learners. Three quarters of all machines sold were less than 150cc. One machine in three was a moped. Only one machine in ten was not Japanese, and fewer than one in a hundred was made in Britain. Yet so great was the grip of Honda on the world motorcycle market that all the machines which the company sold annually in Britain kept its factory in Japan busy for only four days.

3 Motorcycles today

There are well over 200 different models of moped and motorcycle to choose from in the showrooms. As models change regularly, in many cases once a year, the number of different secondhand models is also very large. They range from light mopeds that can do 150 mpg to sophisticated monsters that have engines as large as those of small cars and price tags to match.

Between the two extremes you can find every conceivable combination of size, engine capacity, and engine type. The market is dominated by the four big Japanese manufacturers: Honda, Suzuki, Yamaha, and Kawasaki. Machines are also imported from at least ten other countries – Puch and KTM from Austria, Harley David-

BMW – a sophisticated and expensive machine

son from the USA, Jawa and CZ from Czechoslovakia, Moby-lette from France, BMW from West Germany, MZ from East Germany, Cossack from Russia, Montesa from Spain, and at least a dozen different makes (Moto-Guzzi, Garelli, Gilera, Ducati, etc.) from Italy. Only a few specialized machines are now made in Britain.

While the Japanese companies offer very wide ranges of different machines, the continental manufacturers tend to specialize. Puch is well known for its mopeds, which range from simple 'step-through' models to racy machines capable of comparatively high speeds. BMW makes only large touring motorcycles designed to cruise for mile after mile on motorways where there is no speed limit: they are superbly balanced and comfortable, the Rolls Royces of two-wheelers, and cost nearly twice as much as Japanese machines of similar size and power. Other companies, such as Husqvarna of Sweden, specialize only in off-road machines.

The quality of modern motorcycles is very high. Japanese machines are smooth, quiet, reliable, and on the whole can be described as sweet natured. Maintenance is simple and inexpensive but it *must* be carried out regularly. The same goes for the better-known continental machines. There is little to choose between them, apart from image, styling, personal preference, and price.

With so many different machines available, it is important to choose the right one for the job you want it to do. A nimble machine that buzzes through traffic is not ideal for the open road. A roadster that is comfortable at high speeds on the open road will handle laboriously at low speeds and is not so manoeuvrable for filtering through traffic, so some of the advantages of being on two wheels are lost.

The difference between a town machine and a touring machine can be compared to that between a nippy little car like a Mini and a large limousine. The Mini is ideal in traffic, and will jump ahead of the lumbering limousine. But on the motorway at 70 mph it is running at nearly top speed while the limousine is barely ticking over, with most of its power still in reserve, and it can overtake in a flash. The whole style of driving is also different: one is quick and nervous, the other powerful and relaxed.

In motorcycles the ideal compromise is a machine of about 250cc. This is just as good in traffic jams as a smaller machine but is more comfortable and goes well on the open road, and it is large enough for the rider to discover some of the pleasure that a larger machine provides. In any case a larger machine is not to be recommended unless you have a considerable amount of experience: unless you live in a rural area the weight and power of a big machine can be a handicap for less experienced riders in town driving.

Up to about 200cc most motorcycles have single-cylinder engines. In other words they are driven by only one piston. This might operate on a two-stroke cycle or a four-stroke cycle. There are important differences, which are explained on page 126. Above this size the variety of engine types broadens. A 200cc machine might have a single cylinder, or two cylinders each of 100cc (this is described as a 'twin'). Larger machines have three, four, or even six cylinders. Generally a greater number of cylinders provides smoothness and flexibility, but it also requires more moving parts and these add to the expense.

The next thing to consider is the state of tune of the engine.

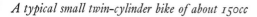

A typical small twin-cylinder bike of about 150cc

Some mopeds, for example, have a top speed of about 30 mph. Others, using the same engine which is tuned up, have a top speed of more than 50 mph. The slower engine is more reliable, requires less service, and is cheaper to run. The more powerful engine is much more highly stressed and so it is more likely to go wrong, needs more servicing, uses more fuel, and is more expensive to buy and to run. Similar comparisons can be made throughout the range of all motorcycles.

In the Suzuki range, for example, the GT380 and the GT500 were recently exactly the same price and both were capable of a top speed of about 105 mph and used roughly the same amount of petrol. But the three-cylinder GT380 developed maximum power at 7,500 rpm (revolutions per minute) while the GT500 twin, a larger engine, developed maximum power at only 6,000 rpm. On the road the smaller machine would feel sportier: you would have to 'buzz' it more, change gear a lot to get the best performance, and in some ways it would be more fun to drive. The larger machine was more gentlemanly: from 30 mph in top gear it would just pull away powerfully and was more relaxing to ride.

In general terms the amount of money spent on a new motorcycle buys a certain top speed. You can get that top speed in two ways. First, with a large engine running slowly, which burns less fuel, is easier to maintain, is more reliable, and is more relaxing to drive. Second, with a smaller engine that is tuned to run more quickly, burning more petrol, is more fickle, and is 'sportier' to drive, which means you have to change gear more often. The sporty machine accelerates quicker but at top speed has to work harder.

There are marked differences between two-stroke and four-stroke engines (for a more detailed technical explanation see page 126). The small two-stroke engine is simple, with very few moving parts, which makes it cheaper to buy. Compared with the four-stroke engine it is more highly stressed and fickle. The two-stroke engine has oil mixed with the petrol and some of this comes out in the exhaust as smoke. The engine seems to run lumpily at idling speeds, coughing and spluttering, while the four-stroke purrs.

When accelerating through the gears the two-stroke engine provides more power but at high speed does not have much in reserve. The four-stroke engine is more of a slogger: it accelerates less quickly but has more pulling power.

In the range of smaller machines (below 250cc) available in Britain today three distinct types are seen on the road – the conventional street bike, the trail bike, and the moped.

Street motorcycles These are by far the most common on the roads today. They are suitable for any road use, whether it is commuting, buzzing around for the joy of it, or touring. The gears and acceleration are adjusted for traffic conditions to provide the best compromise between nimbleness and speed. Tyres are designed to grip on smooth surfaces. All machines that drive on the roads must be fitted with lights, a number plate, and an approved speedometer; but on street motorcycles these are part of the design and do not look as if they have been bolted on as accessories. This type of machine is generally well mannered, easy to ride, and versatile.

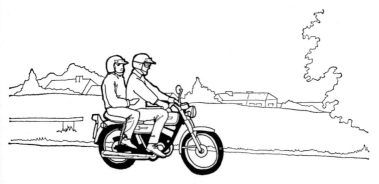

A small single-cylinder Yamaha, a common sight on city roads

Trail motorcycles These are a compromise between cross-country machines and motorcycles made only for road use. Like competition motocross machines they have wheels of larger diameter, very supple suspension, a small and narrow fuel tank, an up-swept exhaust which

A Kawasaki trail bike – not ideal for ordinary road riding

does not touch the ground on corners, and very good acceleration at low speeds.

Trail bikes are fun to ride cross-country – in America campers drive them into the wilds and in Australia and New Zealand farmers use them for rounding up stock instead of travelling on horseback. But like all compromises they must be treated with suspicion. An ordinary trail bike is not good enough to be used in competition, and it is less than ideal for road use.

The characteristically high and wide handlebars, which provide superb control in rough country, are over-responsive on roads. The knobbly tyres, which grip soft ground, wear out more quickly on tarmac than road tyres and do not grip so well in the wet. The lower gears mean that on roads the engine must work harder and therefore wears out more quickly and uses more petrol.

The difference between a trail bike and a roadster can be compared to that between a Minimoke and a Clubman, or a Land Rover and a Rover 2000.

Mopeds   A moped is intended by the law to be a pedal cycle fitted with a small engine of less than 50cc. In countries like Holland, Belgium, and France mopeds are used in great numbers by all types of people for personal transport, and in some cities special lanes are provided for them between the pavement and the traffic lane.

A Puch step-through moped – slow but steady and reliable

Some mopeds are nearer to the bicycle than the motorcycle, with tiny engines that are fitted on the front fork and drive the front wheel by friction. They are as simple to operate as a lawnmower engine and are intended to give a speed of about 20 mph along smooth, flat roads. Others have a U frame, to make it easier for a woman to drive while wearing a skirt, and some are built on the lines of a small motorcycle. Modern machines hardly have to be pedalled at all, except to start the engine, which should not require more than two or three turns of the pedals. Some models have pedals that lock away to provide motorcycle-style foot-rests. Many do not have gears and some have an automatic clutch so all you have to do when moving away is twist the throttle grip.

In general the moped is safe, sensible, reliable, slow, and dull. Around town it provides all the advantages of a motorcycle except speed. But it is by far the cheapest engine-powered transport you can buy, and it is cheap to run – cheaper than travelling by public transport and arguably cheaper than the shoe leather you would wear out by walking.

For young people in Britain the advantage of a moped is that it can be ridden (with only a provisional licence and L plates) from your sixteenth birthday. To ride a motorcycle or drive a car you have to be seventeen. If you already have a car licence, you can drive a moped without L plates and without taking a further test.

The minimum age for motorcycle riding was raised to seventeen in 1972 because the government became concerned at the great number of sixteen-year-old riders being killed or injured. Previously, serious accidents were happening to this age-group at the rate of about six a day. By 1974 that figure had dropped by nearly half. In other words raising the age-limit had saved more than 1,000 sixteen-year-olds from death or injury on motorcycles every year.

What happened, however, was that manufacturers then provided sports mopeds. These were capable of more than 50 mph, they looked and handled like a motorcycle, but legally they were mopeds and could be ridden by people aged sixteen. Although high powered, some did not have very good brakes. As a result the government announced that from 1 August 1977 the maximum speed of new mopeds was to be legally restricted to 30 mph.

Whether the limited speed of a moped is dangerous depends on what kind of rider you are. Many experienced motorcyclists argue that a moped is dangerous *because* it goes slowly. On a moped it can be difficult keeping up with the traffic, so you are constantly being overtaken instead of finding a gap in the traffic and moving along with it. This is certainly true if you are already accustomed to

A Puch sports moped – fast, racy, highly tuned, and expensive

driving a larger machine. The moped's lack of power can be a trap for the unwary.

However, most people who ride mopeds are learners and are more accustomed to riding bicycles. The limitations of the machine are therefore less of a disadvantage. A sixteen-year-old rider can gain valuable experience on a moped before moving on to a bigger machine. It helps you to cultivate awareness and self-control, which are so important. Just as riding a bicycle in traffic is an important nursery stage, driving a moped is an essential intermediate stage. Riding a low-powered moped for a year or so is by far the best introduction to motorcycling.

Handlebars

Motorcycles have a wide variety of handlebars but until you are an expert rider, or are starting racing or scrambling, choose a machine with conventional handlebars. These offer the most comfort and, more importantly, they offer the best control

High and wide handlebars offer superb control when scrambling or trail riding but on the road they are too sensitive; high handlebars are more dangerous in an accident

Drop handlebars let the rider adopt a streamlined riding position and are intended for track racing when little steering is necessary. In traffic they are heavy and difficult for novice riders to handle

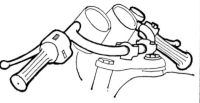

For street use the ideal handlebars are neither low and narrow nor high and wide, but positioned midway between the two extremes so that your body is relaxed and held at a comfortable angle

4   When can you ride?

Legally you do not need any training to ride a moped or motorcycle on the roads in Britain. What you need is a provisional licence and L plates. And you must be the right age – sixteen to ride a moped, seventeen to ride a motorcycle. You cannot ride a motorcycle of more than 250cc until the driving test is passed.

To get a provisional licence for a moped or motorcycle, ask for an application form at a post office, fill it in, and send it with a postal order for the required small fee to the address given. When the licence is received you may put L plates on the front and rear of your machine and drive away. The machine must of course be insured, and taxed, and if it is more than three years old have a test certificate (see page 45).

Mopeds are not allowed on certain roads, such as motorways. You can sit a driving test on a moped, but this entitles you to drive only mopeds and, if you later wish to exchange it for a motorcycle, you will have to sit another test. L drivers are also prohibited from motorways.

As a provisional licence can be renewed for up to three years, the best course is to sit the test on a motorcycle after you have turned seventeen. You are then entitled to drive any motorcycle, including mopeds.

A moped is defined as a cycle powered by an engine of less than 50cc and which can also be pedalled. On some models, however, the pedals are superfluous; they can be removed and replaced by fixed footrests. The machine is then technically a motorcycle.

However, just because you are legally entitled to ride a machine without training does not mean it is a wise thing to do. Riding a motorcycle in traffic without instruction is like playing with a loaded gun. There is nothing difficult about it until something goes wrong. Then it is too late. The whole art of safe motorcycle riding is *avoiding* trouble. But only instruction and experience help you to recognize trouble before it happens.

Unless you are one of the lucky few attending a school that includes motorcycling and roadcraft in its curriculum, getting instruction can be difficult. Motorcycle driving schools, unlike motoring schools, do not exist in every High Street.

Almost the only courses available are run by the Royal Automobile Club and the Auto-Cycle Union. There are 216 RAC/ACU training courses in different parts of the country. The address of a course near to you can be found by asking the local road safety officer (at the town hall or council offices) or inquiring at a police station or RAC office. Some courses have long waiting lists, so, if you plan to buy a machine on your sixteenth or seventeenth birthday, it is advisable to make inquiries and put your name down about six months in advance.

The course costs only a couple of pounds (some are free) and comprises twenty-four one-hour lessons spread over three months. Half the work is done in a classroom learning about the Highway Code, maintenance, and the theory of roadcraft. Half is practical riding on private land where there is no traffic, such as a carpark or council depot. Machines are provided for those who do not have their own, but they usually have to be shared between several people. The test at the end of the course is tougher than the ordinary driving test, but, if you pass it (as most do), you are well prepared for driving on roads.

If you learn to ride by asking another rider to instruct you, make sure that the advice you are given is right. Remember that making the machine stop and start, and learning how to change gear, is only a small part of learning to ride. This has little to do with roadcraft, and it is knowledge and experience of roadcraft that is absolutely essential for safety.

To obtain a full motorcycle driving licence it is necessary to sit a test at the local driving examination centre. The address of the nearest centre can be found by asking at a post office, driving school, or at the town hall.

The driving test is seldom the nerve-wracking experience it is often made out to be. Motorcyclists find it easier than car drivers, because the examiner does not travel with you but stands on the curb and tells you to carry out certain turns and other manoeuvres.

If you know the Highway Code, and can control the machine well and obey the traffic rules, there is nothing to worry about.

The machine must be in a roadworthy condition, and be taxed and insured. The first thing you will be asked to do is to read a vehicle number plate from a distance of twenty-five yards (if you need to wear glasses for this eyesight test, you should keep them on while riding). You must, of course, have a crash helmet.

5   Is motorcycling dangerous?

There is only one answer to this question: yes, motorcycling is very dangerous. More important, however, is another question. Can the dangers of motorcycling be reduced to an acceptable level? The answer is yes – but every rider carries his own safety in his own hands all the time.

The figures speak for themselves. Motorcyclists are killed or injured on the roads at the rate of more than 100 a day. There are several reasons for this alarming figure:

● Although nimble and manoeuvrable, a two-wheeler is inherently unstable. On the basis that the safest speed is zero miles an hour a motorcycle is still potentially dangerous, because it can fall on top of you. The fact that it travels in a position of balance puts it at the mercy of any small thing, such as a patch of oil, which could unbalance it and make it go out of control.

● It is often said that cars, not motorcycles, are most dangerous for riders. The fact that motorcycles are small makes them difficult to see. Many accidents are the result of mistakes made by car drivers, such as failing to see an oncoming motorcycle and pulling out in the belief that the road is clear.

● Acceleration and speed on a motorcycle are exhilarating: many riders drive too fast and have accidents as a result of their own stupidity or recklessness.

● A motorcyclist is completely without protection. A car driver, protected by seatbelts and a steel shell designed to absorb impact by crumpling, can walk away from a quite severe accident. But a motorcycle accident is bound to spill blood and perhaps break bones. If a rider is lucky enough to avoid going to hospital after an accident, he seldom walks away – he limps.

It is foolish and dangerous to pretend that motorcycles are safe, or to suggest that they are as safe as cars. You only have to look at a two-wheeler to see why. It is much better to admit the facts and learn to live with them. When you understand why motorcycles are dangerous, and how accidents happen, you can set about reducing the risks. This must be done in two ways.

First, polish your own driving technique, so that you avoid any accident of your own making; on a motorcycle just one mistake is one too many.

Second, learn to anticipate mistakes that other drivers might make. Presume nothing. Just because a car *should* stop at a halt sign does not mean that it will. In any accident – even one for which you are legally blameless – the motorcyclist comes off worst. With experience you develop a sixth sense, a nose for trouble, which helps you to avoid accidents before they happen.

One reason why so many young people are involved in motor-cycle accidents is that this vital sixth sense has not had time to develop. It takes experience to know that other drivers cannot always be relied upon to do what they should. There is only one way for a young person to drive – as if every other driver on the road, and every pedestrian, is mad. Always expect the silliest and most dangerous thing to happen, and be ready for it. Then, when it does happen, you can avoid the consequences.

This does not mean that you should ride hesitantly. Nervous drivers upset others, making them angry and impatient. Often they cause accidents without themselves getting involved. A motorcyclist must be confident, riding smoothly and firmly but with restraint.

'Am I brave enough to ride fast?' This is not the question that matters. What does matter is whether you are man, or woman, enough to ride with restraint. When it rains, are you sensible enough to slow down and hang back from cars in front? In gloomy conditions or on a shaded road, are you wise enough to realize that your machine might be hard to see and that you should switch on the headlamp? When coming up to an intersection are you thoughtful enough to know that a car waiting at a Give Way sign might pull in front of you without warning?

Restraint is not a quality that young people are expected to have. Everyone thinks that young people are a bit wild, and knows they do things impetuously without thinking. People might complain, but when young people show lack of restraint they generally make allowances. In motorcycling, restraint is not a matter of manners or thoughtfulness. It is a matter of survival.

Most motorcyclists learn this the hard way. If they are lucky, it is just a narrow escape. In fact a bad fright is one of the best things that can happen to a young rider. It is like having an accident without actually getting hurt, but you still learn a lesson that you never forget. If they are unlucky, they get hurt, and have lots of time in hospital to think about the lesson they have learned.

Yes, motorcycling *is* dangerous. But there is no reason why you personally should not be a safe motorcyclist. This comes only with maturity as a driver. It is not something you can buy with the machine, like a luggage rack. You must work at it, think about it, and always be aware of the need for restraint and self control. Look after yourself on the road. Nobody else will.

6 Are *you* safe to ride a motorcycle?

It is natural for parents to have misgivings about their children riding motorcycles. But wanting to ride a two-wheeler is part of a young person's growing up. Most fathers, in their day, have wanted to do the same. On this issue the generation gap is often at its widest and, if it is to be bridged, a great deal of compromise and understanding is required – on both sides.

Winning parents over to the idea is usually the most difficult hurdle for a young person living at home and wanting to ride a moped or motorcycle. Parents argue that motorcycling is dangerous, and they are right. What the young person must do is convince them that he (or she) understands the dangers, then show how he plans to cope with them.

Parents will be impressed by an intelligent approach. If the answer is a firm no, you can only make up your own mind as to how far you can try to change their minds. The first necessity is to convince them that on the road you are a safe, considerate, and responsible character. This cannot be done in a few minutes of persuasion over the kitchen table. It must be demonstrated over a period. Look at your bicycle. Is it well maintained, with brakes in good condition, good tyres, and strong lights? Do you look after it well or is it a bit of a wreck? If you have a history of scrapes and spills, it will be difficult to convince parents that you will be reformed when you have a few horsepower under the saddle.

Some parents worry about the cost of motorcycling. You must show that you have thought the problem through, and that you can cover such things as insurance, road tax, and running expenses. Even when buying a cheap secondhand moped you must be prepared to buy a *new* crash helmet and a pair of stout leather gloves. A protective suit and boots are also important.

Start in a small way. Parents will be reassured if all you want to do at first is buy an old secondhand machine to restore and learn about before you start serious riding. Or, if it is a new machine, they will be happier to see you on a low-powered 'sensible' model until you have gained experience. For young people still at school and bitten by the motorcycling bug, a secondhand moped is an ideal choice.

For young novice riders the RAC/ACU training course (see page 34) is essential. The course is cheap and comprehensive, and you do not need your own machine. If you complete the course and pass the stiff proficiency test at the end of it, all under your own steam, sensible parents are more likely to be impressed that you are careful and responsible enough to ride a machine of your own.

For parents, giving permission to their children to venture out on two wheels is one of the most difficult decisions they have to make. But, if a teenager is old enough legally to drive a moped or motorcycle, parental control is in any case diminishing. Before long they won't have any say in the matter. What parents have is the opportunity to offer practical guidance while they can, rather than merely delay the inevitable by a year or two.

There is a lot to be said for letting modern teenagers do what they want, but ensuring that they do it *well*. In motorcycling this starts with an RAC/ACU training course. Encourage young riders to join motorcycle clubs: it is better that frustrations are worked out in the safety of a scrambling course than in the local High Street.

Most teenagers, particularly boys, would like to ride a motorcycle. Most parents are instinctively dead against it. So it takes a special kind of parent to sympathize with the passion a young person feels for the thing, and to take constructive steps to help him learn about and enjoy it. Some fathers buy motorcycles themselves and ride in company with their sons to begin with. Some buy a motorcycle in their own name and lend it, subject to certain conditions such as dry weather and limited routes. It does no harm to follow a novice rider from a distance, to check his riding ability. A parent who becomes involved in a way that helps a teenager learn to ride properly, and teaches him respect for safety, helps to reduce the risks to an acceptable level.

7 Buying a motorcycle

There is little to choose between the different makes of mopeds and motorcycles. What matters is that the machine should be safe (in the case of a new machine this should not be questionable), that it should 'feel' right, and that it is of a size and type that is suitable for the job you want it to do.

How a machine feels right is hard to explain but is critically important. It is a question of whether you feel in balance with the machine. Do you fit on it as if the whole thing were tailored? When sitting on the saddle you should be able to place both feet comfortably flat on the ground. With the feet on the foot-rests the

For maximum comfort the body should be poised between three points – saddle, pedals and handlebars – with the saddle taking most of the weight

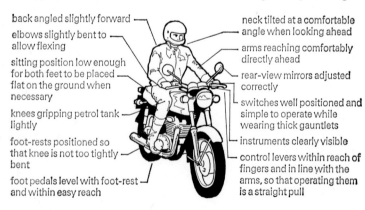

back angled slightly forward

elbows slightly bent to allow flexing

sitting position low enough for both feet to be placed flat on the ground when necessary

knees gripping petrol tank lightly

foot-rests positioned so that knee is not too tightly bent

foot pedals level with foot-rest and within easy reach

neck tilted at a comfortable angle when looking ahead

arms reaching comfortably directly ahead

rear-view mirrors adjusted correctly

switches well positioned and simple to operate while wearing thick gauntlets

instruments clearly visible

control levers within reach of fingers and in line with the arms, so that operating them is a straight pull gear-change lever and brake pedal should be comfortably within reach and you should not have to hold your feet at awkward angles.

You should be able to grip the petrol tank lightly and comfortably with the knees. The arms ought to be comfortably bent at the elbows so the body leans forward slightly but does not strain the back. The arms are control cables, not struts: you should not feel that they are propping you up.

Instruments such as the speedometer must be clearly visible, and all the switches and hand levers should be within easy and comfortable reach. If it is a moped, can it be pedalled easily?

When choosing between the different makes of machine there are three main points to consider. First, find out about the cost and availability of spare parts. Spare parts tend to be expensive, and for models more than four or five years old they are sometimes hard to get. If you are buying a machine two or three years old, and planning to run it for a couple of years, beware.

Check whether there is an authorized dealer near to your home or place of work. What are the public transport connections like? Repairs and servicing are bound to necessitate periodic days in a workshop, so it pays to ensure that it is reasonably accessible.

New machines are supplied with warranties, which vary widely. These are the makers' guarantees. The most common warranty lasts six months (or up to 4,000 miles) for both parts and labour costs. Chains, light bulbs, brakes, spark plugs, and other parts which wear out or have a limited life are not usually included in the warranty.

Motorcycle manufacturers tend to change their models rapidly, usually once a year, and, when the new models come in, most dealers are only too happy to get rid of the old models (which are still brand new bikes) at a considerable discount.

Buying a secondhand machine is much more difficult, because you can only guess at its mechanical condition. If you buy from a dealer, he will no doubt offer some kind of guarantee, but the price will be higher as a result. Buying privately is generally cheaper, but more risky, because you are protected only by your own keenness of eye and thoroughness.

In either case it is important to take along somebody who really knows about motorcycles and can check over the machine for you. It is also better if you tell him how much you can afford and leave him to talk about money with the seller, because he will be much less emotionally involved.

Generally, if a machine starts easily and sounds and looks healthy, it probably is. If a machine looks at all battered or neglected, or if it runs badly, beware. No amount of cleaning can hide rough treatment that a machine has suffered during its life. These are some points to look for:

● If the machine is clean and shiny, does it look as if it has been kept that way, or has it been polished up in your honour? Does it have an air of respectability, or does it look battered and seedy? Bent pedals or foot-rests, or welding repairs to the frame, are sure signs of past trouble.

● Look for rust and corrosion. A good indicator of rough treatment is the condition of the nuts and bolts: if threads are battered, nuts rounded, and screwheads worn, then suspect the worst.

● Spin the rear wheel to see if it runs true, with no wobbles. Look for uneven tyre wear and tread damage. Tap the spokes and listen for any loose ones.

● Rock the wheels laterally to look for worn bearings. Inspect the wheel rims for dents. Are the protruding threads of the axle bolts in good condition?

● Test the chain tension: is it clean and well lubricated, or clogged with grease and grit? Check sprockets for wear.

● Is the steering movement smooth and firm? Rock the machine forwards on the front wheel with the front brake applied: is there movement in the steering head? Lean on the handlebars to depress the front forks then release: the movement should be smooth and easy, with no bouncy rebound.

● Control levers should not be buckled or scratched. Look for frays and kinks in the cables.

● If the battery is in good condition, properly topped up, and with clean terminals, it indicates a history of good general maintenance. Check all light bulbs, switches, and horn and look at the condition of electrical connections.

● Test the oil (if engine is four stroke). If it is clean and in good condition, the engine has probably been well maintained. If it is black and scummy, or containing metal particles, expect a lot of trouble.

● Run your finger beneath the fuel line to look for leaks.

● Start the engine. If it does not start easily and at once, accept no hollow excuses ('She's always a bit temperamental in the middle of the day.') Does the engine idle smoothly? Is the exhaust unduly smoky?

● Let the engine warm up then gun the throttle and listen for vibrations, knocks, and suspicious rumbles in the engine. A slow pick up indicates a dirty carburettor, or worse.

The Department of Environment test certificate (commonly known as the MOT) is required by all machines more than three years old. This covers the general condition of the machine and such things as tyres and brakes and lights. It is intended only to benefit the community at large by keeping dangerous old bangers off the road, and in no sense is it meant to guarantee that the machine is totally safe and roadworthy.

If you are buying a secondhand machine, insist that it has a new test certificate, but remember it is only too easy to doctor a machine so that it passes the test, for example by fitting cardboard brake linings which work once or twice then disintegrate. Although you must have a test certificate, never rely on it.

Accessories

The illustration below shows some accessories you could buy for your machine. When buying accessories, however, it is important to consider what effect they could have on the machine's handling. A windscreen that clips on to the handlebars, for example, might flop about and cause the bike to wobble. The machine is very carefully balanced by the designers and, if you put a large plastic pannier on a luggage rack mounted high over the rear wheel, this could interfere with handling characteristics. According to safety investigators it is safer to protect yourself from wind and rain by wearing a good-quality protective suit and a full-face helmet with visor than to use a windscreen. Safety experts have also found that crash bars protect the engine of the motorcycle if it falls over, and to some extent protect the rider's legs, but in a collision they cause injuries to the shins

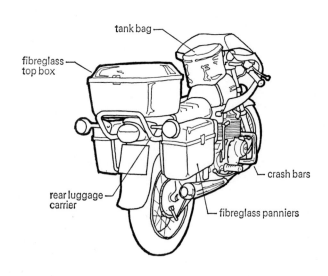

tank bag

fibreglass top box

crash bars

rear luggage carrier

fibreglass panniers

8 Running a motorcycle

Certain documents are required before you can drive away a moped or motorcycle that you have just purchased. Legally you are also required to wear a crash helmet and it is common sense to wear goggles, gloves, boots and a protective suit as well (see page 54).

Provisional driving licence   This is obtained by filling in a form at a post office and paying a small fee. It enables you to ride a moped or motorcycle (depending on the kind of licence) until you sit the test. A provisional licence is not required if you ride a moped and already have a car licence.

L plates   These must be taped securely to the front and rear of the machine if you are driving with a provisional licence.

Insurance certificate   This is proof that the machine is insured in case it injures other people or damages their property (see page 51).

DOE (MOT) test certificate   Required by every bike more than three years old to show that it has passed certain safety checks.

Tax disc   This is the round label which must be displayed in a special holder screwed to the left-hand front part of the machine to show that the road tax has been paid. The amount of tax depends on the capacity of the engine. By 1976 prices a moped or motorcycle of less than 50cc cost £4 a year, a motorcycle of up to 250cc cost

£8, and a motorcycle of 250cc or more £16. It is important to look at the exact cubic capacity, because a so-called 250cc machine might really be only 249cc and therefore fall in the lower price bracket. By comparison, the cost of taxing a car was £40 a year. To renew the tax disc get a form from a post office and send it away to the address given, together with the insurance certificate, logbook, a postal order or cheque for the required amount, and (if necessary) a valid test certificate.

Logbook   The new style of logbook, issued for all vehicles in Britain by a computer based at Swansea, is no longer a green folder but a sheet of paper called the vehicle registration document. It is the motorcycle's passport, because it shows the name and address of the rightful owner. It includes a description of the motorcycle and the numbers of its chassis and engine. Always check these against the document when you take delivery of the machine, whether it is new or secondhand, to ensure that they are correct. Keep the document in a safe place. If you make any changes to the motorcycle, such as painting it a new colour, changing the engine, fitting it with a sidecar, or if you scrap it or change your address, you should fill in the 'changes' section at the bottom of the form and post it to the Driver and Vehicle Licensing Centre at Swansea.

9 The real cost

There are many hidden costs in running a motor vehicle. Whether the vehicle is a car or a moped, it is always more expensive than you think. Not many motorists realize that the real cost of running a modest family car is usually higher than a mortgage on a house. A motorcycle is much cheaper to run than a car, but young people do not usually earn a great deal of money, so they must be equally prepared for the *real* cost of running their own transport.

Costs are in two parts. There are standing costs which remain the same no matter how many miles you ride. Usually they have to be paid only once a year. Depreciation is by far the biggest item and is invisible – you don't notice it until you come to sell the machine and discover how much its value has dropped.

Depreciation is the difference between what you pay for the motorcycle when you buy it and what you get back when you sell it. Generally the bigger and more valuable the machine the higher the depreciation will be. Depreciation is highest during the first year, often as much as 20 per cent. It drops considerably in the second year then levels out. On average you should count on losing about 12 per cent of the machine's value every year.

The second category of costs is the running expenses. This is the cash you pay out of your pocket as you go along – for petrol, oil, repairs, parking. It is amazing how quickly these costs add up during the course of the year.

If the machine is being bought by hire purchase, then the payments you make every year must also be taken into account.

The following table is an example of the real costs of owning and running two different types of small motorcycle and moped at 1976 prices. If you have a machine of your own, use it as a guide for calculating your costs (the table is in round figures):

	New 125cc motorcycle Value: £300	*Moped three years old Value: £80*
Standing charges		
Depreciation at 12%	£36	£10
Insurance	£80 (comprehensive *)	£13 (third party)
Road tax	£8	£4
Test certificate	Nil	£1
	£124	£28
Running costs for 3,000 miles		
Petrol	£36 (60 mpg)	£15 (140 mpg)
Oil	£9	£2
Servicing	£20	£10
	£65	£27
Total cost for year (Add standing charges to running costs)		
	£189	£55
Cost per mile	6·3p	1·8p

* Of course the cost would be reduced if third-party insurance were taken out, but this is not advisable with a new motorcycle costing £300.

10 Insurance

Compulsory insurance protects all road users from financial loss arising from accidents. A driver or rider who is to blame for an accident is expected to pay for repairs, hospital treatment, loss of earnings, and other expenses incurred by the victims of the accident. After a serious accident these costs can reach thousands of pounds. If the driver who caused the accident had no money the victims might never be recompensed.

By taking out insurance you make an agreement with a company to accept the risk on your behalf. You pay the insurance company a fee, which is called the premium. Then, if you are involved in an accident and found to be responsible for damage or injuries that have been caused, it is the insurance company that pays.

The advantage of this system is that, if you happen to be the victim of an accident that was not your own fault, you will always receive proper compensation – not from the person who caused the accident, but from his or her insurance company. Obviously it is very risky indeed to drive without insurance. Not only are you breaking the law, but if you do cause an accident you might have to pay a great deal of money in damages.

The agreement between the insurance company and yourself is called the policy. There are several different kinds of policy. According to the law, the only policy you *must* have is a 'third party' policy to cover any damage you might do to other people or their property.

To cover damage caused to your own machine take out a

'comprehensive' insurance policy. This will pay for any repairs, and, if the machine is so badly damaged that it cannot be repaired, the company will pay the full value so it can be replaced by another of the same type and age.

In most comprehensive policies the first few pounds' worth of damage are not included. This amount, which is agreed at the time you take out the policy, is called the 'excess'. Its purpose is to protect the insurance company from small claims arising from minor scratches and scrapes. For young riders a typical excess is £25. In other words, you pay the first £25 worth of damage from your own pocket. The excess reduces as you get older and become more experienced. A thirty-year-old motorcyclist with a good record need pay no excess, unless he volunteers it to reduce his premium.

A third type of policy is called 'third party, fire and theft'. It covers the machine against damage that might be done to other people, and against loss or damage as a result of fire or being stolen.

The number of insurance companies that issue motorcycle policies is small compared with those that deal in car insurance. Every company has its own system of assessing risk, so premiums vary a lot. It is worthwhile contacting several different companies to ask for a quotation, so that you can find the best deal.

Alternatively get in touch with a recognized insurance broker who acts as a middle man between clients and companies and will know which company to approach. The names of local insurance brokers can be found in the *Yellow Pages* and most have offices in the local High Street. Approach only those who are members of one of the professional organizations – the Federation of Insurance Brokers, the Association of Insurance Brokers, or the Corporation of Insurance Brokers.

Not surprisingly, young motorcycle riders with little or no previous experience on the roads are not considered by insurance companies to be good risks, so premiums tend to be high. The more powerful the machine and the younger the rider, the higher the premium.

A moped is relatively cheap to insure, but a young novice rider pays twice the premium of an experienced rider with a good record.

As soon as you buy a bigger machine the premium makes a big jump. Third party insurance for a 125cc motorcycle ridden by a seventeen-year-old is four times higher than for a moped. Comprehensive insurance could be 60 per cent higher again.

If you buy an expensive and high-powered machine as soon as you get your full motorcycle licence at the age of seventeen, it may be difficult to find insurance at all, but, if a company did give you comprehensive cover, the cost could be well over £150.

Insurance premiums are higher for comprehensive policies, more powerful machines, younger riders, and city driving. Premiums fall as you grow older, get more experience, if you live in a rural area, or if you drive a low-powered machine.

After the first year of claim-free riding most companies give a discount on the next year's premium. This increases year by year until, after four years, the maximum discount is about 25 per cent. Then, if you do have an accident and make a claim, you start again by paying the full premium.

Motorcycle insurance policies differ from car policies in several important ways:

● Theft of accessories and personal belongings from the machine is not covered unless the whole bike is stolen.

● Medical expenses and personal accident benefits are not included; to get these you have to take out a different policy.

● In most cases you are not covered when driving other motorcycles, particularly if your own machine is less than 100cc. Before driving another motorcycle look carefully at the wording of the policy. Also the policy probably does not cover damage caused to your machine by other riders.

The insurance certificate, which proves that the machine is insured, should be kept in a safe place with the vehicle registration document. If stopped by the police you may have to produce it, or show it at a police station. It is a good idea to make a photocopy of the certificate to carry around with your driving licence.

11 Togging up

The simple rule of getting dressed for a motorcycle ride is that the more skin you cover the less you lose. Even in dry and sunny conditions a motorcyclist should be dressed for the job. Gloves are essential to protect the hands, which in an accident are extremely vulnerable. A shirt of strong material with the sleeves rolled down, or a stout jacket, protects the arms and back. Jeans or leather trousers are ideal: never wear shorts.

Shoes are safe enough for commuting and short-distance travel in town, but plimsolls and sandals offer no protection at all to the feet. For serious motorcycling a pair of strong leather boots that

The right gear for fine weather

- goggles
- crash helmet
- stout wind-proof jacket with long sleeves
- strong gauntlets or gloves long enough to cover wrists
- trousers of strong material
- bright colours for safety
- wet-weather suit carried on luggage rack
- leather boots big enough to take thick socks

come halfway up the calf, big enough for you to wear thick woolly socks inside them, are essential. For cross-country riding they should have 'slipper' soles with smooth heels that cannot catch on the ground.

In wet weather no place is as windy and as wet as the saddle of a motorcycle. But staying dry and warm is essential for safety, because you have to be relaxed and alert. A strong waterproof suit made of waxed cotton keeps you dry in the rain, stops your street clothes from getting dirty, and provides a certain amount of protection from skin abrasions if you come off. Getting in and out of a motorcycling suit is not quick and easy, but it is worth doing.

A motorcycling suit should be big and baggy to go over your ordinary clothes. If the material goes tight over the knees when you bend your legs your knees will get cold and the blood circulation to the feet may be affected. Openings in the suit – leg and wrist cuffs, front and neck – must be capable of being worn tight, to keep the water out. The front zip must be protected by a weatherproof flap. The collar should be high, with room for a towel to be worn underneath.

The right gear for wet weather

- goggles or visor (visor protects entire face from stinging rain)
- crash helmet
- high collar tightly fastened
- towel around neck
- belt or elasticated waist prevents flapping
- loose-fitting trousers which do not go tight at the knees
- trouser cuffs that do up tightly over boots
- sleeve cuffs that do up tightly and tuck into long gauntlets
- layers of thin clothing beneath suit are warmer than single garments
- in very wet weather plastic bags worn outside or inside boots help to keep feet warm and dry
- weather-proofing flap keeps water and wind out
- if suit is two-piece, coat should have good overlap
- bright colours for safety

Some suits have zip-in woolly linings for winter use, which means that they must be extra large. Nylon suits are the most convenient. Waxed cotton is more durable and waterproof but the wax tends to collect dirt and come off on your finger nails; however, the material can be reproofed when necessary.

Leather suits are very comfortable and offer good protection in an accident, but they are not waterproof and the rain soaks into the leather so that it becomes heavier and heavier until you feel you are wearing a wet-suit for skin-diving. The suits are tailored to be comfortable in a riding position and the leather has to be 'worn in'. Like boots and gloves, leather suits should be treated with leather dressing to replace natural oils. Leather clothes that do get wet should be allowed to dry out slowly: if put in a hot place, the leather will crack and harden.

Gloves should be comfortable with the hand slightly clenched, as if holding the handlebar grips, and there should be no wrinkles on the palm. If gloves are too tight blood circulation to the fingers might be affected, so that you get pins and needles or go numb. If too loose they might interfere with the safe working of controls. A big pair of gloves or gauntlets can be made more comfortable and more suitable for the job if a thin pair of cotton gloves is worn inside them. Nylon gloves or mitts are inclined to slip on the controls.

Driving a motorcycle without goggles or visor can lead to permanent eye damage. Insects and stone chips are a constant hazard. At 50 mph raindrops drive into your face like needles. The wind pressure on your eyeballs causes pain and watering which becomes uncomfortable and can affect vision. A crash helmet visor or a good pair of goggles with safety glass (laminated glass is best of all) is essential.

Always keep the lenses or the visor well polished and replace when scratched or you will be dazzled by direct sunlight and on-coming headlights. Soften dirt particles with water to avoid damage when rubbing them off. Special goggles are available for those who wear spectacles, or you can buy goggles with corrected lenses fitted so that they can be worn in place of spectacles. A crash helmet visor protects the whole face from wind and flying objects, and raindrops are brushed away by the slipstream, and therefore 'wipers' are not necessary. Goggles and visors can be tested for distortion by holding them at arm's length and looking through them.

On a motorcycle with a windscreen the wind and rain will be deflected from the front but the turbulence will suck rain behind you and your back will get cold and wet unless you take the precaution of wearing warm and waterproof clothing with no gaps.

12 Why wear a crash helmet?

A human head weighs about ten pounds. When your body stops abruptly from a speed of 5 mph the head effectively weighs five times as much. From 20 mph it weighs twenty times as much, or 200 pounds. If you run into the side of a stationary car at that speed, it will have the same effect as hitting your head with a 200-pound hammer. If you are the kind of person who believes in hitting your head with that kind of force, then don't bother to wear a crash helmet when you ride a motorcycle.

In fact it is compulsory to wear a crash helmet. If you do not do so, you can be charged by the police and fined by a court. But it should not be merely the fear of getting caught that makes you put on a helmet every time you ride a motorcycle or moped – *without fail*.

The head is the most vulnerable part of a person. It can be injured at very low speeds. While a broken arm will mend in a week or two, an injured brain could make you a cabbage for the rest of your life.

A motor car is an extremely uncomfortable object to hit at any speed, because it has so many jagged edges. If you hit the side of a car, your body slides along the petrol tank of the motorcycle and your face smashes into the top of the car door – where there are sharp edges such as the roof gutter, the top of the window, and perhaps a roofrack.

If you hit a car head-on, the motorcycle stops dead and your body continues travelling forwards, in a sitting posture, at the same speed as before. The legs hit the crash bars and the thighs hit the handle-bars. This can cause severe injuries. The body is tilted forwards, so that now you are hurtling through the air head-first, almost horizontally.

You might dive head-first through the windscreen of the car, or you might slide over the roof. But it is more likely that your head will hit the sharp edge of the roof at the top of the windscreen. It is like hitting a knife-edge – not a blunt one, because fragments of windscreen shattered by your head can be rather sharp.

Direct-impact accidents like these are the worst kind and even at speeds as low as five or six mph can cause considerable damage. If your head is protected, however, you stand a much better chance of surviving without any permanent damage.

When you fall off a motorcycle at speed, as a result of skidding or being touched by a car or hitting a pedestrian, your body hurtles forwards and is slowed only by the friction of the things it touches – usually the road surface. It has been described as an experience that rounds off all your square corners!

Accident investigations have shown that the body does not slide smoothly along the road but bounces. First you hit the tarmac two or three times, then you might hit the curb, then a telegraph pole or a parked car. In this kind of accident the head bangs against a solid object on average *seven* times. Any one of these blows could cause severe head injuries, which a crash helmet would help to prevent.

When wearing a crash helmet, the head is protected from shock in several ways. First, the purpose of the helmet is to distribute the shock over a wider area of the head, but to do this effectively it must fit properly. Second, it is designed to absorb impact. It does this partly by destroying itself. This means that after an accident a crash helmet cannot be relied upon and should be replaced.

All crash helmets are made to strict specifications and in Britain they may not be sold unless they bear the 'kitemark' of the British

Standards Institution. Samples of every batch of helmets made are tested in a special laboratory to prove that they meet the laid-down standards.

Crash helmets sold in Britain (even those made overseas) must comply with British Standard BS5361, which was introduced in July 1976. The old standards, BS2001 and BS1869, were phased out at the end of 1976. New helmets are now all of the 'jet' type which protects the temples, ears, and the lower part of the back of the head. The old-fashioned 'pudding basin' type may still be worn, but it is illegal to sell them, because they no longer comply with the standard.

A fourth type of helmet made to BS2495 is designed for motor racing and it has to meet additional specifications such as resistance to fire. For any kind of speed competition on motorcycles, including scrambling, helmets bought with an 'ACU approved' label must be worn. These helmets have been tested to additional specifications. All BS2495 helmets are also ACU approved.

A crash helmet should fit comfortably on the head, allowing a little room because the head tends to swell when it gets hot. When you put it on and shake your head, the helmet should not slide more than about a quarter of an inch. You should be able to open and shut your mouth comfortably while wearing the helmet, which should sit squarely on the head.

It must be securely fastened by a strap under the jaw. Some helmets also have a chin strap, but it is illegal to use this alone, because the strap will not prevent the helmet from coming off in an accident.

There are two styles of helmet in use. One is cut away to leave the face open. This is the cheaper and more common type for general motorcycling. A peak can be clipped to the front to shade the eyes, or you can fit a visor of clear moulded plastic that drops down to protect the whole of the face from the wind.

A more expensive type is the 'full face' helmet which fits over the entire head like a streamlined diving helmet and has an opening cut for the eyes, nose, and mouth. This type is extremely strong

A full face helmet   *An open face helmet*

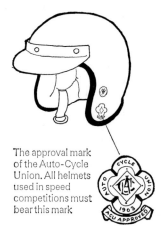

The British Standards Institution Kitemark— do not buy a crash helmet without it. The number refers to the standard to which the helmet is made. BS 2495 is the specification for racing helmets. BS 5361 is the new specification for helmets for ordinary use

The approval mark of the Auto-Cycle Union. All helmets used in speed competitions must bear this mark

because the bar protects the chin and offers valuable reinforcement. Remember:

● Buy a *new* helmet, the best you can afford.

● Buy only a helmet with a BSI kitemark.

● Replace a helmet that is bumped hard.

● Do not hang a helmet by its harness.

● Always fasten the helmet by a strap under the jaw.

● Sweat can rot the stitching, so check the harness regularly.

● Beware of painting the helmet, because certain paints can set up a chemical reaction a̶n̶d̶ ̶w̶e̶a̶k̶e̶n̶ ̶t̶h̶e̶ ̶s̶h̶e̶l̶l̶

13 See and be seen

See and be seen is survival rule number one. Motorcycle riders must always be aware of the fact that other drivers may have difficulty seeing them. A motorcycle with its rider has only a quarter of the frontal area of a car. Much of it is not distinct – the front tyre, engine, driver's face. Other drivers look out for other cars and lorries – vehicles which are bigger than their own. They often forget to look out for motorcycles and they sometimes genuinely do not see them coming.

It is up to the rider, therefore, to make himself *be* seen. The visibility problem occurs at all times, not just in rain or at dusk, but in full daylight and mainly on urban streets.

In daylight wear bright clothing such as a fluorescent 'safety orange' waistcoat. On a light-coloured concrete road remember that light clothes are as difficult to see as black clothes on tarmac.

A headlamp cover of fluorescent safety orange is also valuable, but, if conditions are at all dull, do not hesitate to remove the cover and switch the headlamp on dipped beam. This is bright enough to be seen for a long way and it will not dazzle other drivers or run down the battery. A sidelight or parking light is useless for any form of driving – you only have to look at parking lights used by other vehicles to see how weak they are.

At night always use a headlamp – on dipped beam in towns, on full beam on the open road when there is no oncoming traffic. Reflective tape stuck on your helmet, the back of your jacket, and the backs of your gloves (to make hand signals more visible) is also useful.

Remember – in motorcycling, dull is deadly.

Ten ways to make yourself visible on the road

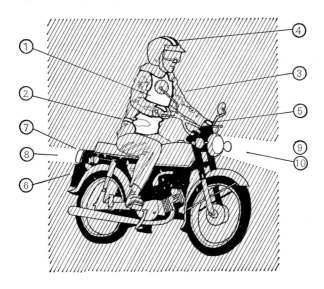

1 Safety-orange fluorescent waistcoat
2 Reflective belt
3 Brightly coloured clothing (colours neither pale nor dark)
4 Reflective tape on back of helmet
5 Reflective tape on backs of gauntlets
6 Reflective rear number plate
7 Red reflectors
8 Check that all lights are working, particularly rear light and stop light
9 Safety-orange fluorescent headlamp cover for daylight use
10 Use headlamp (without cover) on dipped beam at night and in daylight when visibility is bad

II Control and roadcraft

1 Ride the police way

Riding a motorcycle safely and well is an art. Like anything worth-while it is not a skill you can pick up as you go along. It has to be thought about, and learned. Later, when you are familiar with the basic principles, your own style of driving will emerge.

Riding safely does not mean that you are chicken-hearted. Far from it: anybody can ride fast and dangerously. But it takes a real expert to ride safely and know when it is safe to increase speed, when it is wise to hold back.

Police motorcyclists are high-speed professionals. They are specialists at combining maximum safety with optimum speed. Instructors at the Metropolitan Police Driving School in London are masters of the art of safe riding. The following section on motor-cycle control and roadcraft is based on the system they have per-fected through many years of experience.

The skill of the police motorcyclist is rooted in system and awareness. First, he recognizes a hazard for what it is. Then he puts into practice a certain procedure. The procedure is a simple three-point rule:

Before the hazard is reached be:

- in the *right* position;

- travelling at the *right* speed;

- in the *right* gear.

In order to recognize the hazard in the first place you have to look a long way ahead – and think. The moment you stop thinking, trouble will happen. No matter how powerful his machine or how good its brakes a motorcyclist's only protection from an accident is his own alertness. Once that switches off he is in trouble.

Police motorcyclists are schooled in what Scotland Yard calls 'The Ten Commandments of Motorcycling'. These are the fundamental rules of safe riding:

1 *Ride according to the Highway Code* and you will ride safely and well. You can't expect to ride safely if you don't know the rules of the road.

2 *Concentrate at all times and you will avoid accidents.* This is the key to good riding: it ensures skilful handling and prevents mistakes such as late braking.

3 *Think before you act.* Do not ride automatically but think out every move in advance. Anticipate what other drivers might do, so that you can be ready to avoid them. Always think of the unlikely thing that could happen.

4 *Hold back when necessary.* Follow other vehicles at a safe distance and do not overtake unless you can complete the manoeuvre in safety. A motorcycle is not a bulldozer.

5 *Ride with deliberation.* Be firm, not hesitant or uncertain. The decisions you make must be quick and correct.

6 *Use speed intelligently.* Ride fast only in the right places. Any fool can ride fast enough to be dangerous. The maximum speed permitted is not always safe.

7 *Develop machine sympathy.* The motorcycle should feel like an extension of your body. Drive it without jerks or vibration. This reduces wear and makes you a better rider because, if you understand the engine, you will always be in the right gear.

8 *Give proper signals.* This helps other road-users because, if

your intentions are plain, they will be able to keep out of your way. Use the horn thoughtfully.

9 *Ensure your motorcycle is roadworthy.* Defective machinery, bad brakes, or worn-out tyres are killers.

10 *Perfect your roadcraft.* This is the art of avoiding awkward or dangerous situations. It prevents accidents and makes riding less of a strain.

Safety check Your life may depend on a one-minute safety check of every machine you ride. It should be carried out every day without fail. See page 154 for weekly checks.

- Are the tyre pressures correct? (Check when cold.)

- Check tyres for flints, uneven wear, tread depth.

- Are all light bulbs working, including the rear light and the brake light?

- Are any control cables loose or beginning to fray?

- As you move away check brakes – do they work smoothly and firmly?

- Is there petrol in the tank? Check oil level of engine.

2   Sitting properly

The way you sit on a motorcycle and operate the controls says a lot about your ability to ride well. Do you *look* as if you are in control?

You should be at ease in the saddle, not hunched up or stiff. Movements should be smooth and unhurried, not jerky or flurried. The way you handle the machine should be effortless. It should not be a struggle, or appear that you are not quite in charge.

Sit tidily: as soon as the machine begins to move bring the feet up and put them on the foot-rests. Do not drag them along or let them hang out. When stopping, you should not have to put a foot down until the last moment. Watch a police motorcyclist stop at traffic lights: he drives slowly up to the white line in low gear, stops, *then* puts a foot out.

Control and balance at crawling speeds is more difficult than at faster speeds. Practise riding the machine slowly in tight circles, or in figures-of-eight round obstacles. Keep the feet up at all times. Travelling at less than walking pace a good rider can turn from lock to lock without losing balance or putting a foot down.

You should be able to find and operate all controls and switches with your eyes shut. It is dangerous to look down at the gear-change pedal while in motion. Put the machine on its centre-stand, sit in the saddle, and practise the different operations with the engine off. While looking ahead can you put your hand immediately on the ignition key, reserve petrol tap, light switches, indicator switch, dip switch, and horn?

A motorcycle seems strange after riding a bicycle because the weight distribution is different and you sit much nearer the ground. There is a knack even to simple things like putting it up on its stand, and this should be mastered before you go out on the roads.

3 Accelerating

There are two good tests of acceleration sense. How far can you ride without using the brakes? How long can you follow another vehicle while staying exactly the same distance behind?

The real skill of acceleration is knowing how to use just enough. When moving away from a standing start accelerate smoothly and resolutely, neither racing the engine so that it screams and vibrates, nor letting it struggle. Ease the gear-lever through the gears, don't stamp it.

Blipping the throttle while sitting at a red traffic light revs the engine unnecessarily, making noise that irritates other people, wastes petrol, and wears out the engine.

There are three grades of acceleration:

1 *Delicate*   This is just enough throttle to pull the machine along at a steady rate without increasing speed. It is used for controlling the machine on a tight bend, or on a wet road.

2 *Normal*   When you want to increase speed unhurriedly, in ordinary driving, this is just enough acceleration to get the machine moving at a gentle rate.

3 *Firm*   This is used when you want to get going in a hurry, but the machine must be upright (that is, not banked in a corner), the road dry and straight with no dangerous camber or slippery patches.

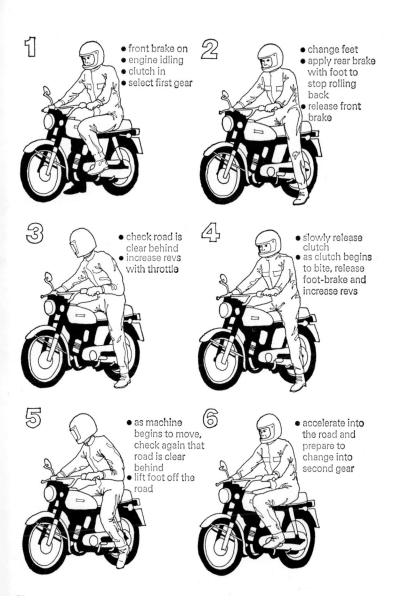

1
- front brake on
- engine idling
- clutch in
- select first gear

2
- change feet
- apply rear brake with foot to stop rolling back
- release front brake

3
- check road is clear behind
- increase revs with throttle

4
- slowly release clutch
- as clutch begins to bite, release foot-brake and increase revs

5
- as machine begins to move, check again that road is clear behind
- lift foot off the road

6
- accelerate into the road and prepare to change into second gear

How to accelerate away properly from a standing start on a hill

Unnecessary acceleration causes a great deal of expensive wear on tyres and chain. It also uses a lot of petrol and wears out the engine besides leading inevitably to unnecessary braking which wears out the brakes and also adds wear to the tyres.

Brisk acceleration is fun on a motorcycle. Up to about 50 mph you can leave sports cars behind. When overtaking other vehicles,

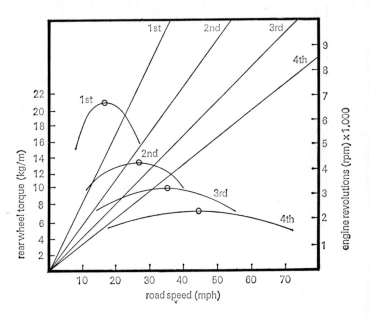

The engine performance of a small Japanese two-stroke. Close reading of this chart shows when you should change gear to obtain maximum acceleration. The torque curves show when the engine is exerting the most effort on the rear wheel. The secret of quick acceleration is to change to the next gear when the torque begins to fall off. In this example:

1st gear: Up to 6,800 revs (18 mph)
2nd gear: Up to 4,200 revs (27 mph)
3rd gear: Up to 3,200 revs (35 mph)
4th gear: If revs fall below 2,000, change down to 3rd gear

firm acceleration used wisely is a positive advantage because you can get quickly through the danger zone.

With experience you develop an ear for the engine note and can tell instantly when the engine is labouring (and you need to change down a gear) or over-revving (and you need to change up a gear).

When accelerating hard, it is not the power of the engine that counts so much as the 'torque'. This is turning effort on the crank-shaft that is available for propelling the motorcycle – it is the 'oomph' that makes the thing go. Maximum torque is usually found about halfway up the range of engine rpm, so staying in one gear until the machine will not go any faster than changing gear is not the quickest way to build up speed.

The amount of torque that the engine exerts can be plotted on a graph and this is printed in most owner handbooks. If your machine has a tachometer (rev counter), and you have studied the torque curve, you can change gear at the point when the torque begins to fade. Then commence accelerating in the next gear at the revs at which torque is near its peak. This means that the engine is always kept pulling at its absolute best as you go up through the gears.

4 Braking

Braking is never easy. It takes more skill to brake quickly and tidily than to travel fast. The reason is that when brakes are applied the motorcycle loses much of its natural stability. Also, the area of rubber in contact with the road is not much greater than the ball of each foot and this has to take all the strain without skidding.

In a car there is only one brake pedal and you do not have to worry about how much force to apply to the front and to the back. But a motorcycle has two brakes. The handlebar lever works the front brake and the foot pedal works the rear brake. The rider must decide for himself the best combination of force.

On dry roads with a good surface most of the stopping power is in the front wheel because the weight of the machine and rider is thrown forwards. So you squeeze hard on the front brake and tread more lightly on the rear brake.

If the rear brake only is used, it takes a great deal longer to stop and causes a lot of wear on the tyre. If the rear wheel locks, its braking power is lost: always keep the wheels turning. Locked wheels cause skids.

When the road is slippery the front brake must be applied more gingerly. If the front wheel were to lock or skid, a crash would be inevitable. The braking effort must be divided equally between front and rear. This means that the motorcycle takes longer to stop, so on slippery roads you have to drive more carefully, slow down, and brake earlier.

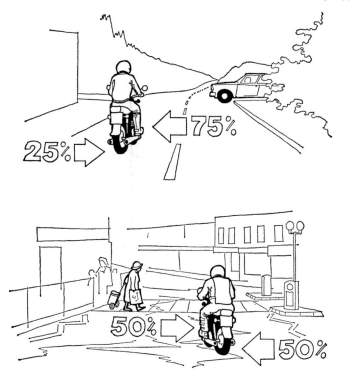

The relative proportion of front and rear brake you should apply in (top) *dry conditions and* (bottom) *wet conditions*

Brakes must be applied firmly but not fiercely. Like accelerating, braking should be a smooth operation with no sudden jerks and no fuss.

In a car you can change down a gear and use the engine to help slow you down. This is not good practice on a motorcycle because it has the same effect as applying only the rear brake. The effect is that the rear wheel is dragged along and bounces, perhaps causing loss of control. Brake first. Then change down into the appropriate gear for negotiating the next hazard.

The five rules of sensible braking are:

1 Brake only when the machine is upright and travelling in a straight line.

2 Use both brakes in conjunction with the gears.

3 Select the best part of the road for braking – dry and rough surfaces are best, so keep your eyes open.

4 Braking on a bend is dangerous. If you must brake on a bend, you have made a grave mistake and can only make the best of it. Apply the rear brake lightly, never the front brake.

5 Do not use the front brake when turning, banked over, or on a road made slippery by ice, gravel, oil, or wet leaves. On a wet road use it gingerly and only when the machine is upright and straight (remember a damp surface is more slippery than a really wet one).

5   Stopping

Applying the brakes in the right way is only a small part of stopping a motorcycle. The other part is the real art. In itself, stopping is not difficult. The hard part is: can you stop *in time*?

If a lorry in front suddenly claps on its brakes for seemingly no reason – can you stop before running under its rear end?

If you drive round a blind bend and find a combine harvester straddling the width of the road – can you stop before you are corn-flaked?

If a taxi ahead does a U-turn without warning, as taxis often do – can you stop before hitting it?

The secret of being able to stop quickly enough to avoid a collision is to be always ready, always looking for the unexpected. You must hang back and give yourself room to stop. But how much room do you need?

Few drivers properly understand just how long it takes to stop a car. At 70 mph the stopping distance is longer than a football pitch. In wet or slippery conditions it could be twice as long.

First you must allow for your own reaction time. This varies between different people. Just over half a second is a good reaction time, but the normal is nearer to three quarters of a second. If you are day-dreaming, the delay before you begin to brake could be much longer.

At 30 mph you cover the ground at the rate of 44 feet every second. So in the best conditions a rider with good reactions covers 30 feet before his foot and hand reach the brake controls. This thinking time is about one foot for every mile an hour.

Then the brakes begin to work. But the faster the speed of the machine the longer it takes to stop.

From 30 mph the brakes should pull the motorcycle to a halt in about 45 feet. The total stopping distance is therefore the thinking distance plus braking distance – 75 feet. This is the length of road taken up by six average-sized cars parked nose to tail.

At 50 mph the stopping distance is 50 feet to think and 125 feet to brake – a total of 175 feet, or fourteen cars parked in line.

At 70 mph the overall stopping distance is 315 feet, longer than a football pitch – equivalent to twenty-seven car lengths.

Remember, these stopping distances are only the *best* you can expect. They depend on quick reactions, good brakes, good tyres, and dry roads. When the road is wet or if the brakes are a bit dodgy, the stopping distances are much longer.

In dry conditions motorcycle brakes are about equal to those of cars. But many small machines, particularly mopeds, sports mopeds, and small motorcycles, have bad brakes. According to the Transport and Road Research Laboratory the braking distance of an average car travelling at 30 mph is 40 feet. But a conventional moped stops from 30 mph in 53 feet, a sports moped in 55 feet, and some 90cc motorcycles in 61 feet. Reaction times must be added to these figures. Inexperienced riders and commuters who ride smaller machines must therefore be doubly alert.

The sensible general rule is this:

● Up to about 30 mph, when you can see past the car in front and the road is dry and clean, allow at least 1 foot per mile an hour between yourself and the car in front.

● Over 30 mph, or when the vehicle in front blocks the view ahead (as a lorry does), allow at least 1 yard per mile an hour.

6　Cornering

Bends are favourite sites for accidents. From a motorcyclist's point of view every bend is an accident waiting to happen. The usual cause of trouble on bends is too much speed. When you ride into a bend too fast, two things can happen.

You run out of road, swing wide, and hit something such as an oncoming car or an object on the roadside (if it's only a grassy bank you are lucky: it might be a stone wall). Or you come across an unexpected obstruction such as a traction engine, or a broken-down caravan, and you can't stop before hitting it.

If you drive into a corner too fast you have made a serious mistake. A motorcyclist is not allowed to make mistakes. Now you have got to pay for it. This may sound sinister, but it is true.

Like any other hazard encountered on the road, remember the police system – position, speed, gear: before going into the bend the machine should be in the right position, travelling at the right speed, and be in the right gear.

A blind bend must obviously be taken more slowly, and in a lower gear, so that you can stop if necessary. When there are wide verges and you can see the road ahead, you can go faster but nevertheless should keep a good look out for other dangers such as oncoming traffic, slippery surfaces – wet leaves or spilt oil – and potholes that might cause you to swerve.

The sharper the bend the slower you should be travelling *before* reaching it. It is dangerous to brake on bends. So you must do all your braking, and change down into the right gear, before you reach it.

Then go round the bend under gentle acceleration. Go at a constant speed, neither gaining speed nor losing it, so that the engine pulls you gently round. Only as the bend straightens out and you can see the road ahead while the machine comes upright should you increase speed again.

By positioning correctly on the approach to a bend, you can make it less sharp. Before a left-hand bend start near the crown of the road (if it is safe to do so). Turn into the corner early so that there is a safety margin before you inadvertently drift over the centre line.

For a right-hand bend start as near as possible to the left so that you can see round the corner. Then turn into it late to come out of the bend positioned near the crown of the road (if it is safe to do so).

The dangers of swinging wide on a bend are obvious. But, if you are travelling at the right speed and in the right gear, you should be able to:

1 Stop within the length of road you can see.

2 Position the machine anywhere on your side of the road without difficulty.

One important factor to consider when sizing up a bend ahead is the camber. This is the angle of the surface of the road. Some corners are banked like a race track so you can drive around with almost no steering movement.

On public roads, however, corners are often cambered adversely. Far from helping you to stay on the road, the angle of the road tends to throw you outwards. This type of bend must be recognized well in advance and taken much more slowly.

When a road is humped in the centre, for rainwater to run off each side, the effects of the camber change on different bends. On a left-hand bend the camber works for you, having the effect of a

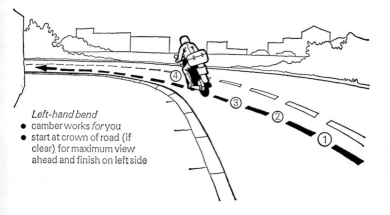

Left-hand bend
- camber works *for* you
- start at crown of road (if clear) for maximum view ahead and finish on left side

The correct way to take bends

1 Be in the right position
2 Size up the sharpness of the bend and any other dangers, and adjust speed well in advance, braking while the machine is upright
3 Select the right gear
4 Gentle acceleration around the bend at constant speed

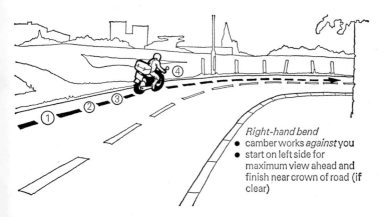

Right-hand bend
- camber works *against* you
- start on left side for maximum view ahead and finish near crown of road (if clear)

banked track, but on a right-hand bend the camber is against you and needs to be taken more slowly and in a lower gear.

Roundabouts   Roundabouts present motorcyclists with at least five hazards in one – plus the dangers of other traffic and always the risk that other drivers will not give way when they should.

1 The approach road is highly dangerous, being polished by use and impregnated by rubber from wheels being braked; when dampened by a shower of rain it becomes as slippery as ice. Be in the right position, and travelling at the right speed, and in the right gear before you reach it.

Hazards at a roundabout

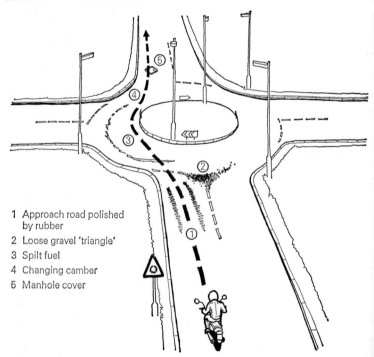

1 Approach road polished by rubber
2 Loose gravel 'triangle'
3 Spilt fuel
4 Changing camber
5 Manhole cover

2 Loose gravel often accumulates in the centre of the carriage-way.

3 Petrol and diesel fuel tends to slop out of tanks of other vehicles on sharp corners like roundabouts, and engines of vehicles stopped at the give-way line tend to drip oil.

4 Look out for changing camber while going round the round-about.

5 Also look out for objects such as manhole covers, and broken glass, or objects that have fallen from lorries.

When there is no other traffic, the safest route through a roundabout is the straightest one. With other traffic around be careful to stay in your own lane and use the indicators as recommended in the Highway Code.

7 Positioning

The Highway Code says that all vehicles should be driven as near as possible to the left side of the road. This is not always the best position for a motorcycle.

Being small and narrow, a motorcycle has more choice in the matter than a car. A car can deviate only a foot or two because it occupies nearly the full width of the carriageway, but a motorcycle may be driven near the gutter or near the crown of the road.

With more of the road to choose from, the rider must know which is the *best* position.

The correct position in all situations is the one that provides the best possible view of the road and other traffic. And it is the one which gives other drivers the best chance of seeing you.

Nearer the crown of the road the motorcyclist has better visibility at junctions, can see ahead beyond parked cars, is visible to oncoming traffic, and can usually find a safer road surface free from diesel fuel and gravel.

But you should not be so close to the centre-line that oncoming traffic is alarmed or obstructed. And it is important to keep a close watch on your rear-view mirror to ensure that you are not blocking traffic coming up from behind.

Another aim of good positioning is to have space in front of your machine – space in which to stop if necessary. Instead of following directly behind another vehicle it is better to hang back and (1) move towards the centre of the road so that you can look ahead along the

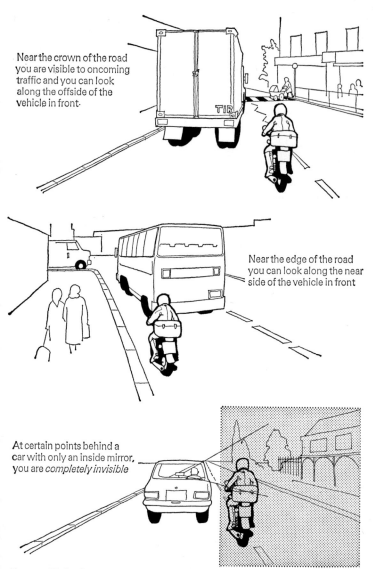

Near the crown of the road you are visible to oncoming traffic and you can look along the offside of the vehicle in front.

Near the edge of the road you can look along the near side of the vehicle in front

At certain points behind a car with only an inside mirror, you are *completely invisible*

Always think about your position on the road

off-side of the vehicle in front, or (2) take up a position nearer the gutter so that you can look ahead inside the vehicle in front.

Only when you hang back, and position yourself so that you can look ahead and see what the vehicle in front is likely to do, can you plan an escape route if something unexpected happens in front.

Don't hide behind other vehicles then suddenly weave out into the centre of the road, as if from nowhere.

Be aware of other drivers' blind spots. If the car in front does not have an outside mirror you will be invisible if you ride on the outside, near the centre-line. The danger then is that he might look at his inside mirror to see if the road is clear then turn right without signalling because he does not know you are there.

● Think about what you can't see.

● Think about what other drivers may not see – can they see *you*?

8 Turning

Turning can be dangerous because other drivers may not be alert enough to realize what you are doing. As soon as you do something different from everybody else in traffic you are in a risky situation.

First, the turn must be considered like any bend in the road. The machine must be in the right position, travelling at the right speed in the right gear, before beginning the turn.

Look out for the usual dangers found on bends, such as bad road camber, wet leaves, oil on the road, or loose gravel.

Secondly, think about what you might encounter after you have made the turn. Are pedestrians about to cross the road? Are people likely to open the doors of parked cars? If there is a pedestrian crossing, it might be slippery or require you to stop.

But the biggest danger when turning at road junctions is other vehicles. A motorcycle is vulnerable because it is small and hard to see. When a rider slows down in traffic, or stops on the crown of the road to make a right turn, he must be alert for any other driver who seems to be blind.

The danger is worst at night. The single red light of a motorcycle travelling more slowly than the rest of the traffic, or stopped in the middle of the road until it is clear to turn right, is hard to pick up against a maze of moving red tail lights. Flashing indicators are particularly useful in the dark because they indicate your position to other traffic.

Always look over your shoulder at least twice before making the turn. Once to see if the road behind is clear. The second time just

1 Slowing down, signalling, changing into the right gear for the turn

2 Following vehicle sees your signal and moves to the left, to pass along your near side

3 Second following vehicle realizes this is an opportunity to overtake; its driver has not seen your signal and does not know your intentions

4 As the second vehicle accelerates forwards, you turn unwittingly in front of it—CRASH!

How not *to* **turn right**

before turning. This is what police riders call 'the lifesaver'. It gives you a chance to accelerate forwards to safety if a following driver has not spotted your signal, or is not aware that you have slowed down in his path.

A left turn at a junction is nearly always a sharp one. Drive more slowly, in a lower gear. Glance over your left shoulder just before turning. Watch for cyclists on the near-side.

When making a left turn out into a busy road always stop until the road is clear: never join the traffic without warning, even if there is room near the kerb, because this can alarm other drivers and cause them to swerve, possibly causing an accident.

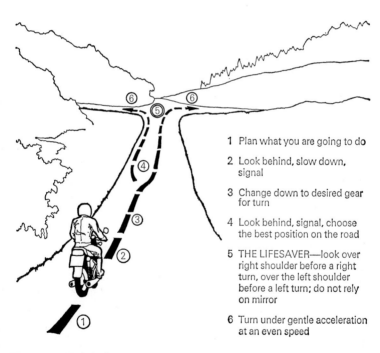

1 Plan what you are going to do

2 Look behind, slow down, signal

3 Change down to desired gear for turn

4 Look behind, signal, choose the best position on the road

5 THE LIFESAVER—look over right shoulder before a right turn, over the left shoulder before a left turn; do not rely on mirror

6 Turn under gentle acceleration at an even speed

How to turn correctly

9 Overtaking

When overtaking spend as little time as possible in the danger zone. The danger zone is the area where:

1 You are coming up close behind the vehicle in front.

2 You are alongside the other vehicle (does its driver know you are there?).

3 You are on the wrong side of the road.

It is better to hang well back from the vehicle in front until the road is clear then accelerate up to it and overtake quickly. This gives you time to pick up speed before swinging out into the danger zone. And you get through the danger zone quickly.

If you first pull out from behind the other vehicle, then begin to accelerate, you spend longer in the danger zone.

Also from a position well back you have a better view of the road ahead. This can be particularly important when following a lorry.

Overtake decisively. Hesitation when overtaking is dangerous. It is a matter of vision, position, judgement of speed and distance – and decision.

First, move to the left and look along the near-side of the vehicle ahead to ensure that there are no hazards such as parked cars or pedestrians which could make it swing out.

Then move to the crown of the road and look outside the vehicle in front to see if the road is clear. Signal, and look behind to ensure that it is safe to pull out.

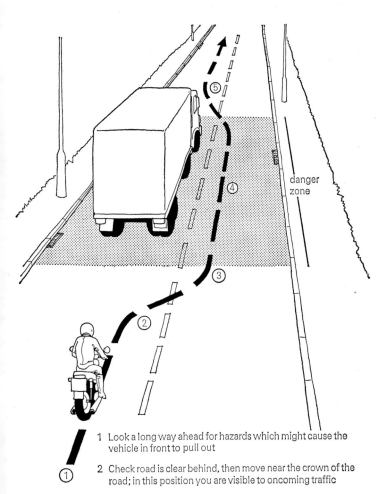

danger
zone

1 Look a long way ahead for hazards which might cause the vehicle in front to pull out

2 Check road is clear behind, then move near the crown of the road; in this position you are visible to oncoming traffic

3 When it is clear to overtake, begin accelerating, signal, and check behind; sound the horn or flash the lights if the driver may not have seen you

4 Give overtaken vehicles as much clearance as possible to avoid turbulence

5 Return to left side of road as soon as possible

The safe way to overtake

Accelerate briskly. Give the vehicle in front a wide berth. Lorries and coaches create a lot of turbulence which can affect a motorcycle. Return to your own side of the road as soon as possible.

Give the driver in front warning of your intention by a flick of the lights or a toot on the horn if you suspect that he has not seen you. Do it thoughtfully, however, and remember that the horns on most machines are weak and cannot be heard in a lorry or car going at speed with the windows up.

Do not overtake:

1 Unless you are absolutely certain it is safe to do so.

2 On a corner or bend.

3 At a road junction of any kind (including intersections on dual carriageways).

4 On a blind brow of a hill.

5 When there is a solid white line in the centre of the road, or a no-passing line.

6 When approaching a pedestrian crossing, or when a vehicle ahead is stopped at a crossing.

7 In a narrowing roadway or when approaching roadworks.

8 When approaching a hump-back bridge.

9 When approaching a level crossing.

10 Approaching gateways or entrances to cafés, factories, service stations, or building sites from which traffic might emerge suddenly.

10 Filtering

According to the Highway Code you must not jump the queue at traffic hold-ups. But the whole advantage of riding a motorcycle or moped on busy roads is its small size that enables it to buzz past crawling cars and lorries.

The intention of the rule is that drivers should act considerately. A car that tries to barge ahead of the queue is clearly not being driven with consideration, because other drivers must hold back to let it in.

But a motorcycle is able to filter through queues with reasonable safety and without delaying other drivers. A motorcyclist can take advantage of existing gaps where cars cannot fit.

Much depends on the size and power of the machine you ride. A small machine will slip through narrow gaps more easily but, when traffic begins to accelerate away, as from traffic lights, it may not have the power to get ahead and is more easily boxed in by fast-moving cars.

Overtaking a line of stopped or slowly moving traffic is satisfying, as every rider knows. But it also has dangers.

A car driver stopped in a queue at a red light might suddenly decide to get out to remove his coat, or adjust his windscreen wipers. Passengers in cars stopped at junctions often take the opportunity to get out.

The edge of an opening car door is a sharp and uncomfortable object to hit at any speed. Worse than that, however, is the fact that

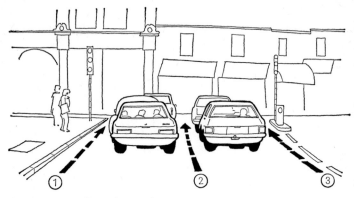

1 The ideal route if there is enough room
2 Filtering between two lines of cars is unwise but frequently done; be doubly alert for opening doors and ride very slowly. Find a gap before traffic begins to move
3 Only if there is plenty of space at the front of the queue and no oncoming traffic

4 Weaving between cars like this is inconsiderate and unwise

Good and bad ways of filtering through stationary traffic

your instinctive reaction is to swerve away from it. You could hit an oncoming car head-on.

When overtaking lines of traffic, drive slowly, expect the worst to happen at any second, and leave as much room as possible for doors to open without warning. Switch on your headlamp.

There are other dangers too, such as drivers who suddenly decide to do a U-turn or change lanes, and drivers who put an arm out of the window to knock out a pipe. Watch for pedestrians dodging through the traffic, particularly at night when they are hard to see.

Beware of moving alongside long lorries that could trap you as they turn left. Stop behind a vehicle, where its indicators are visible, rather than alongside. Be on the alert when coming up to cars trying to edge into the traffic stream – their drivers are looking for gaps, not motorcycles, and may suddenly dart out.

11   Defensive riding

Awareness is a motorcyclist's only protection. Alertness and observation by themselves are not enough. To be aware you must be alert, and observant, and you must *think*. This is the only way to develop the kind of sixth sense that lets you know when another driver is going to make a mistake.

A motorcycle rider is at every other driver's mercy. Scrambling across the countryside or speeding around a race-track he might be the best motorcycle rider in the world. But in traffic those skills are worthless unless they are combined with awareness.

Awareness means:

● Knowing exactly what is happening all around you, including behind.

● Allowing for every other person to act like an idiot at any moment, and being ready.

● Being in firm and precise control of your own machine at every second, so that you can cope with any situation.

What this adds up to is a technique called defensive riding. Its aim is totally selfish. It is the policy of every rider who knows he is at the mercy of everybody else. Defensive riding is the method he adopts for protecting himself. If he does not look after himself, nobody else will.

Safe motorcycling is largely a matter of technique that can be learned and practised. Many aspects of the correct technique have been covered in this book. But safe motorcycling is also an attitude of mind. This is not so easy to learn from a book. It must be developed through experience. Only experience gives you a sixth sense that rings some kind of mental alarm bell just before another driver does something stupid.

Young riders have no opportunity to get the right kind of experience without jumping in at the deep end, so to speak. As a result they are often involved in accidents for which they are legally without blame.

Other people refer to them as 'accident prone', but this is misleading and wrong: young riders are involved in this kind of accident only because they have not had time to develop the art of defensive riding.

When a car is seen approaching a junction from the left a motorcyclist might see the Give Way sign and say to himself, 'that car should stop'.

An inexperienced rider therefore believes he is in the clear and takes no precautions.

But a rider who knows about defensive driving asks the important question, 'that car should stop, *but will it?*'

If the car does not stop, the young rider smashes into the side of it and is carried away on a stretcher. He is blameless. And hurt.

The experienced rider, however, takes the precaution of covering the brakes just in case they are needed, and when the worst happens he is able to pull up in time. He might be angry. He has certainly been wronged. But he is not lying in an ambulance.

Some of the clues to look for when riding defensively are obvious when you think about them, others are less so.

No motorcyclist has a right to be surprised, for example, when a bus halts at a bus stop. Buses and bus stops go together. In the same way, other combinations can help you forecast what other vehicles will do.

A caravan is likely to turn into a caravan site. A council truck is likely to do anything strange when approaching roadworks. Lorries are attracted by roadside cafés. Beer lorries and breweries go together, as do brick lorries and brickworks, or brick lorries and building sites. Taxicabs might do anything.

On the following pages are examples of defensive riding – and how to develop a nose for trouble.

Character reading   You can tell a lot about a driver by looking at his vehicle:

1 Hot cars – the old saloon car with wide wheels and tiny steering wheel, and covered in accessories and stickers, shows an enthusiastic driver who is likely to cut you up just to show how much cleverer and better he is – motorcyclists might be the best drivers but they have the worst accidents. Look out for jutting radio aerials

2 Delivery vans – they are liable to stop suddenly or swerve to the other side of the road

3 Drivers with spectacles – they have a blind spot level with and just forward of their shoulders; so, if you are running abreast of a car driven by a driver with spectacles, you may be invisible.

4 Battered banger — steer clear of dented cars because they sometimes show drivers with bad records of careless and thoughtless handling; the next thing they dent might be you

5 Nodding dogs and dancing dolls — these are dangerous distractions and indicate drivers who do not know the importance of unobstructed visibility; what else don't they know?

6 Foreign cars — drivers abroad have different habits from British drivers; if a passenger is map-reading, don't be surprised by a sudden stop or change of direction

7 Bad maintenance — cars with wobbling wheels, flapping mudguards, bad suspension, bald tyres, or spluttery engines are a menace and betray drivers who might be equally casual about the condition of their brakes. Badly loaded lorries are also a menace — things often drop off

Pedestrians In an accident with a pedestrian the motorcyclist usually comes off worst. A sudden swerve to avoid a pedestrian can take you into the path of an oncoming vehicle. Sudden braking can lead to loss of control. Motorcycle riders should be rather more careful of pedestrians than should car drivers.

1 Buses – watch for passengers jumping off the rear platform as the bus slows down, people walking out from in front of the bus when it is stopped, and people running across the road to catch it as it begins to move

2 Ice cream vans and school gateways are danger-spots for children – approach with caution, ready to brake

3 Pedestrian crossings – people often walk straight out without waiting, and it is the driver's responsibility to be ready to stop. When stopping for a pedestrian do not flash lights as a signal but give the slow-down signal

4 Stationary traffic – pedestrians crossing through the traffic can step out from in front of high vehicles into the paths of motorcycles filtering towards the head of the queue

5 Baby carriages – mothers often push a pram ahead of them when crossing a road; when she is stepping out between parked cars the mother's head and shoulders might be visible but the baby carriage hidden

6 Dogs – if a dog runs across the road, look for another one because they often play in pairs. If chased by a dog, never swerve but let the dog keep out of your way

Signalling

1 Don't hesitate to use the horn (except at night in built-up areas) to inform other drivers or pedestrians of your presence. A short toot is kinder than an angry blast and may save an accident.

2 Indicators on a motorcycle are often indistinct because they are mounted so close together. From a distance, especially at night, a motorist cannot be certain whether the rider is planning to turn left or right, but they do indicate his position. Use flashers in addition to hand signals.

3 A quick flick of the headlight is often helpful, particularly on fast roads, when the horn may not be audible. Use it to inform another driver of your presence, not as a demand to be let by. In slow traffic it usually means, 'I am giving way'.

4 Other drivers sometimes signal that the road ahead of them is clear for you to overtake. They may do this by waving you on, or briefly switching on the left indicator. This is helpful, and should be treated as an invitation to pass. It is not an order. Always satisfy yourself that the road really is clear.

Passing parked cars Riding alongside a row of parked cars can mean trouble for the motorcyclist who does not keep his eyes peeled. Give parked cars as much clearance as you can, though this is not always possible when other traffic is overtaking. Be alert for the following clues which could mean that (a) a car door will open; (b) a vehicle will pull out in your path.

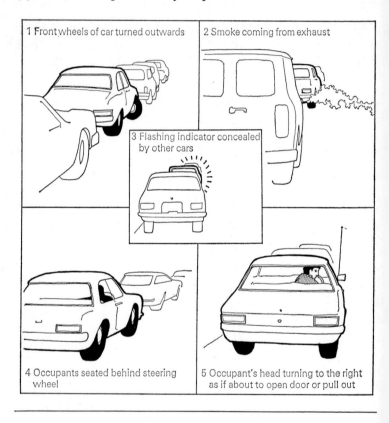

1 Front wheels of car turned outwards

2 Smoke coming from exhaust

3 Flashing indicator concealed by other cars

4 Occupants seated behind steering wheel

5 Occupant's head turning to the right as if about to open door or pull out

Slippery surfaces A motorcyclist must always 'read' the road ahead – gauging the amount of grip that the surface provides for the tyres and adjusting speed accordingly.

Roads which look smooth and shiny, as if made of polished steel, can be slippery even in dry weather, and after a shower of rain they are positively lethal.

This is because rubber dust engrains the tarmac during fine periods and when moist it turns the road into a skid-pan. For this reason skids are more frequent in summer than in winter. Heavy rain washes the surface clean.

In general, suburban streets tend to be more slippery than open roads, which are sometimes treated with non-skid compounds. Heavily used roads collect a gloss of oil.

Rain also conceals slippery patches, such as areas of polished or oily tarmac. Wet leaves lying on the road can be as slippery as ice. White lines can be slippery when wet, and so can pedestrian crossings.

Ice is dangerous enough if you are in a car. For a motorcycle ice is positively murderous. Avoid it at all costs, even if you have to ride all the way at a few miles an hour with the wheels in the gutter to get a grip.

A sure sign of ice is when all tyre noise on the road suddenly stops and you feel as if you are gliding. All you can do is try to remain upright and straight. Do not apply the brakes or the wheels will lock and you will go completely out of control.

Oil collects on roads outside garages, at traffic lights on busy routes, at bus stops, on roundabout approaches.

Watch for irregularities on the road surface which can throw you off course – thick white lines, railway lines, manhole covers, tarmac ridges. Cross them at right angles rather than obliquely if you can.

Tractors often leave tracks of greasy mud. And watch for gravel falling off lorries, and on newly surfaced roads.

Riding at night

1 Use a dipped headlamp which stands out but does not cause dazzle; do not rely on a sidelight

2 In moving traffic a motorcycle side-on is practically invisible, so beware of turning in front of moving vehicles or stopping on the crown of the road to turn right

3 When a car approaches do not look at its headlights but at the near-side of the road. Oncoming lights often silhouette obstacles such as pedestrians and parked cars

4 On the open road, when there is no other traffic, dip the headlight at a left-hand bend to illuminate the nearside verge; at a right-hand bend use full beam

5 Wear light-coloured clothing with reflecting tape or fluorescent material

6 Dazzle can be reduced by ensuring that visor or goggles are absolutely clean and not scratched. Do not wear tinted goggles or visors at night

7 Always drive within the limits of your lights so that you can stop if necessary – it is better to slow down than to hit an unlit steamroller or builder's skip

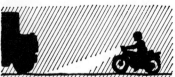

8 Beware of a single oncoming light – it looks like a motorcycle but it could be a car with one bulb not working

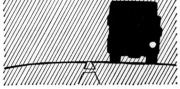

Country riding Some of the hazards are shown below. Do not rely on warning signs and remember that local people familiar with the road drive that little bit faster than is wise.

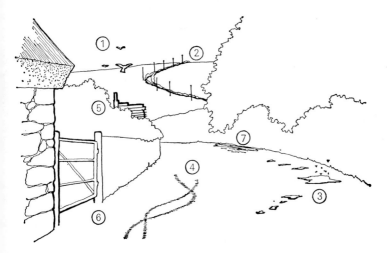

1 Birds flying up from a hidden part of the road may indicate an oncoming vehicle

2 Telegraph poles and hedges can indicate the trend of the road but sometimes you can be misled by them

3 Cowpats and mud on the road can be slippery, and indicate that tractors or livestock are about

4 Skid marks on the road show that other drivers have been misled – slow down, there's something tricky ahead

5 Tractors and other machines travel slowly, and slow speeds are often very difficult to judge. On narrow roads a milk lorry or combine harvester can be nearly as wide as the road, so be ready to stop

6 Watch out for strong gusts of wind blowing between farm buildings and wall openings

7 Be careful approaching a heavily shaded section of road such as a cutting, or a small bridge in a hollow, where ice might be found

12   Pillion riding

Riding the pillion of a motorcycle is fun if you have full confidence in the driver. If you don't have confidence, don't do it. L-drivers are allowed to carry only passengers who themselves hold full motorcycle driving licences.

Like the driver, the pillion rider must wear a good crash helmet and be dressed in bright protective clothing. With the driver's body for protection from the slipstream the coldest part of the anatomy is usually the back.

Sit in a relaxed way: don't try to fight it when the machine is banked over in a bend. Don't try to bank the machine over before the driver is ready. Just move with the machine. The driver should hardly notice the pillion-rider's presence.

1 Wear bright protective clothes similar to those of rider
2 Crash helmet is required by law
3 Keep feet on the foot-rests which should be comfortably positioned so that if necessary you can 'rise in the stirrups'
4 Take a firm grip of rider or machine
5 Keep your head still
6 Do not give hand signals
7 Do not put feet down when machine stops at traffic lights

The feet must be placed on proper foot-rests (these are required by law) and the weight evenly distributed between the foot-rests and the saddle. Take a firm grip on the machine or the driver's hips. Your body should not overhang the machine.

When mounting the machine keep one foot on the ground until you are seated: do not stand on the foot-rest and swing a leg over as if getting on a horse. Do not take your feet off the rests when the machine stops at traffic lights.

It is important that all driving is left to the driver. Never give hand signals. Don't keep trying to look ahead and wriggling your head about because this is disconcerting.

III Know your machine

A motorcycle is only as good as its rider. Unless the rider has a working knowledge of its mechanics and knows why it behaves in certain ways, he (or she) can hardly expect to control it well or get the best out of it.

This section describes how a typical small motorcycle operates. Styling and layout and many details differ widely between models and types of motorcycle, so it is important to read this section in conjunction with the owner's handbook. The basic functions of the different mechanical components are broadly the same from bike to bike.

Small engines operate very fast and need constant maintenance to prevent them going wrong. Do-it-yourself maintenance is cheaper and teaches you about the machine, but it must be regular and thorough.

Many jobs, such as wheel alignment and brake adjustment, are very simple, but it is important to remember that they are critical to your own safety. If you do not feel confident about doing the work yourself, don't risk it, but have the work done by an expert mechanic.

Most mechanical repairs can be done in a home workshop if you are prepared to work at it, but it pays to get hold of a workshop manual for your model of machine (most libraries have them) before you begin dismantling anything complicated.

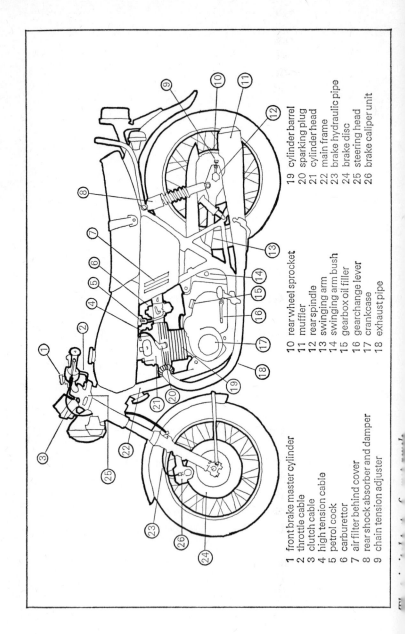

1 front brake master cylinder
2 throttle cable
3 clutch cable
4 high tension cable
5 petrol cock
6 carburettor
7 air filter behind cover
8 rear shock absorber and damper
9 chain tension adjuster

10 rear wheel sprocket
11 muffler
12 rear spindle
13 swinging arm
14 swinging arm bush
15 gearbox oil filler
16 gearchange lever
17 crankcase
18 exhaust pipe

19 cylinder barrel
20 sparking plug
21 cylinder head
22 main frame
23 brake hydraulic pipe
24 brake disc
25 steering head
26 brake caliper unit

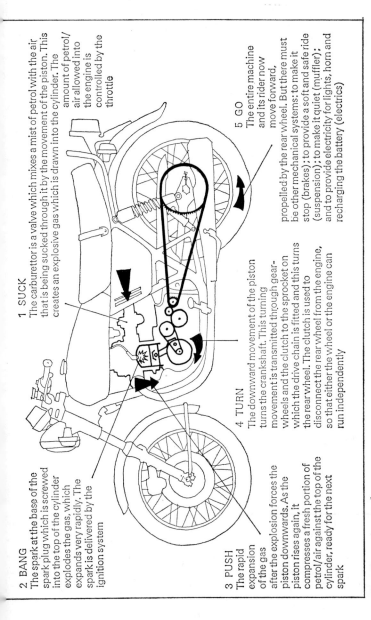

1 SUCK

The carburettor is a valve which mixes a mist of petrol with the air that is being sucked through it by the movement of the piston. This creates an explosive gas which is drawn into the cylinder. The amount of petrol/air allowed into the engine is controlled by the throttle

2 BANG

The spark at the base of the spark plug which is screwed into the top of the cylinder explodes the gas, which expands very rapidly. The spark is delivered by the ignition system

3 PUSH

The rapid expansion of the gas after the explosion forces the piston downwards. As the piston rises again, it compresses a fresh portion of petrol/air against the top of the cylinder, ready for the next spark

4 TURN

The downward movement of the piston turns the crankshaft. This turning movement is transmitted through gear-wheels and the clutch to the sprocket on which the drive chain is fitted and this turns the rear wheel. The clutch is used to disconnect the rear wheel from the engine, so that either the wheel or the engine can run independently

5 GO

The entire machine and its rider now move forward, propelled by the rear wheel. But there must be other mechanical systems: to make it stop (brakes); to provide a soft and safe ride (suspension); to make it quiet (muffler); and to provide electricity for lights, horn and recharging the battery (electrics)

How the engine works

1 Suck + bang + push + turn = Go!

A motorcycle engine is rather like a three-dimensional Chinese puzzle. Each piece of the puzzle is a different mechanical or electrical system. The pieces are complicated in design and by themselves don't make much sense. But they are finely engineered to slot together to make a compact mechanical unit that carries you along the road at a twist of your right hand.

Each of the pieces in the puzzle has its own job to do:

The carburettor draws in petrol and air and mixes them together into an explosive gas (suck).

The ignition system makes a spark which causes the gas to explode and expand rapidly (bang).

This forces the piston downwards (push).

The downward movement of the piston makes the crankshaft go round and this is transmitted to the rear wheel (turn).

Result: the machine begins to move forwards.

Each of the four main pieces of the puzzle which do these jobs has its own support system, such as the battery or magneto which supply the electricity that makes the spark.

At its simplest the working of a small engine can be described like this: suck + bang + push + turn = go!

The whole process happens at once, very rapidly. When the engine is idling it happens about 1,000 times a minute. At full speed it happens well over 7,000 times a minute.

Also the whole process is complementary. The turn of the crankshaft makes the electricity for the next bang. The push of the piston creates the suction that drags petrol and air into the carburettor.

What happens when you kick the starter, or press the button, is that you set everything going. After a revolution or two the engine will take over and run on its own accord.

The four main functions of the engine, and the systems that support them, are described in more detail on the following pages.

2   Carburettor

The carburettor is a delicate instrument mounted on the side of the engine. Its job is to mix petrol with air. This forms a highly explosive vapour which is drawn into the cylinder by the piston, is compressed, and then ignited by a spark.

Inside the carburettor is a circular flap or slide, which swivels to open or close the main passage. This is called the throttle and its job is to regulate the amount of petrol/air reaching the cylinder. It is controlled by the twistgrip on the right handlebar, to which it is connected by a cable.

The carburettor in position on a machine

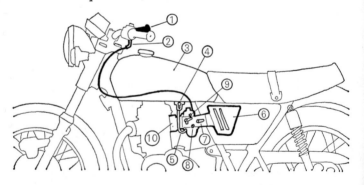

1 throttle twist grip	6 air cleaner
2 throttle cable	7 coldstart lever (choke)
3 petrol tank	8 air screw
4 petrol cock	9 throttle stop screw
5 petrol supply line	10 cylinder inlet

The twistgrip does the same job as the accelerator pedal of a car. To make the engine work faster a movement of the twistgrip opens the valve in the carburettor and more petrol/air reaches the cylinder where it goes off with a bigger bang and creates additional power.

Air reaches the carburettor by way of the air cleaner, which traps any dust that might clog the delicate and narrow pipes and jets.

Petrol is delivered to the carburettor by gravity when the petrol cock (tap) beneath the tank is turned on. It runs into a chamber at the base of the carburettor where there is a float that controls the amount supplied. As petrol in the chamber is used up, the level drops and the float falls, allowing more petrol to flow in from the tank above.

The basic operation of a carburettor is quite simple. As air is sucked in it must pass through a narrow tube, called the venturi. To get through the constricted space it must travel faster. As it passes over a narrow spout, called a jet, it sucks petrol up from the chamber below.

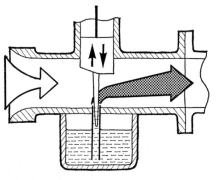

Air sucked through the narrowing tube must go faster; it draws petrol from below and the two mix to make an explosive vapour

A simple carburettor

But the job is made more complicated by the need to vary the mixture of petrol and air for different jobs and different running speeds. When starting from cold the engine needs a very 'rich' mixture with lots of petrol and not much air. When cruising or idling, it requires less petrol and the mixture can be 'lean'.

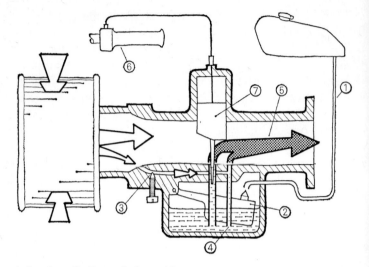

1　Petrol supplied by gravity from tank
2　Float automatically keeps petrol level constant
3　When engine is idling, air enters through this narrow passage which can be adjusted by air screw
4　Petrol is sucked up by way of the pilot jet
5　The petrol/air mixture is drawn into the cylinder
6　When the twistgrip is turned, it lifts the slide
7　As the slide is drawn upwards, it allows more air to enter and also lifts the tapered needle that has been shutting off the main jet and this lets in more petrol

How a carburettor varies the mixture

The carburettor varies the mixture from one third petrol when starting to about one sixteenth petrol when cruising, and it does most of this automatically. The rider has to worry only about operating the twistgrip to make the machine go faster or slower.

The simple carburettors fitted to most small motorcycles do this with additional passages. When the engine is idling, air is drawn through a special channel and the main channel is closed by a sliding throttle valve.

This slow-running channel connects with the pilot jet. It supplies just enough petrol and air to keep the engine ticking over sweetly.

The engine is made to idle faster or slower by turning the pilot screw which opens or closes the jet opening.

When the throttle is opened it lifts the slide, allowing air to roar in by way of the main air channel. Below the slide is a needle that fits into the opening of the main jet. As the slide rises it also lifts the needle, so that the increased air flow can suck out more petrol.

When a very rich mixture is required for starting the engine from cold, a lever is operated by hand. This might be mounted on the carburettor itself, or be connected by cable to a lever on the handle-bars. It does the same job as the choke in a car. Either the air intake is partly blocked, so that more petrol is sucked in, or a special jet which bypasses the others is brought into use.

As soon as the engine is warm the coldstart or choke lever should be returned to the normal running position. Too much petrol in the cylinder makes the engine run roughly and can cause damage and unnecessary engine wear.

Use only the grade of petrol recommended for your engine. Low-octane petrol (two or three stars) is intended for less exacting or low-compression engines and is cheaper. High-octane petrol (four or five stars) is for high-performance engines. Using a low octane in a highly tuned engine causes damage, and using a high octane in a low-compression engine is simply a waste of money.

3 Ignition

As the explosive mist of petrol and air is sucked into the cylinder from the carburettor it is ignited by the bright flash of the spark plug. The spark is produced by a pulse of electricity surging down the inner core of the spark plug. At the bottom it is confronted by a gap. Like Evel Knievel speeding down a ramp it can do only one thing – jump. When electricity jumps it makes a spark.

An efficient ignition system is essential for reliability and good performance. But, while many motorcyclists are mechanically minded, the ignition is often a mystery to them, and neglected. The consequence is that it often gives trouble.

Cars and large motorcycles make electricity with a dynamo or alternator. These are turned by the engine and the current is used to recharge the battery, which supplies other components, including the ignition system.

Small motorcycles usually have a flywheel-magneto system which delivers electricity direct to the ignition, electrical components, and to the battery. The magneto is just a small and very simple type of generator. Coils of fine wire are mounted inside the flywheel, which is turned by the crankshaft. The flywheel is heavy and its main purpose is to smooth out the running of the engine. It is also fitted with magnets. When these spin around the coils of fine wire, an electric current is generated in each of them.

The current for the ignition system comes from one of the three coils. But, like water trickling out of a garden hose, it has volume but no strength. Without strength it cannot jump and make a spark.

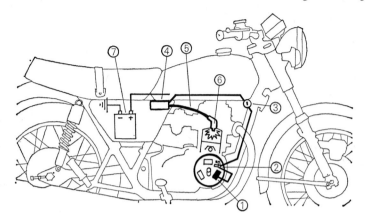

1 Flywheel magneto is turned by the crankshaft and makes electricity
2 Contact breaker opens and shuts rapidly as the engine turns, momentarily interrupting the current
3 Ignition switch breaks the circuit when the key is turned off and stops the engine
4 Each time the contact breaker interrupts the current the high-tension coil creates a strong pulse of electricity
5 The high-tension lead carries the spurt of high voltage from the coil to the spark plug
6 Jumping across the electrodes at the bottom of the spark plug the strong electric current creates a spark, igniting the petrol/air and causing it to explode
7 The battery is also connected to the magneto and together they provide power for lights, indicator, horn, etc.

How the spark reaches the cylinder

Somehow the current must be made to 'squirt' – the way one squirts water by putting a finger over the end of the hose.

This is done by the high-tension (HT) coil, which is mounted under the saddle or sometimes in the magneto itself. Inside the HT coil are two windings of fine wire. The weak current passing through one of them sets up a powerful magnetic field in the other. When the current is switched off the magnetic field collapses and creates a powerful surge of current. The surge travels down a special wire (the high-tension lead) to the spark plug.

To create a succession of sparks – several thousand a minute – the current must be rapidly switched on and off. This is the job of the contact breaker, which is usually fitted beneath the flywheel. The contact breaker is made to open and shut by a revolving cam. Its two tiny metal surfaces, which touch then part to make and break the electrical circuit, are called the points.

The condition of the points is always critical. They must be regularly cleaned and adjusted so that the clearance between them is exactly correct. If the points are dirty, the current is obstructed and, if they do not open sufficiently, they become pitted.

The spark reaching the cylinder must be bright and strong. Also it must arrive at the split instant when the mixture of petrol/air is fully compressed by the upward stroke of the piston. The faster the engine turns the earlier the spark must arrive.

The timing of the ignition is critical. Setting up the timing is complicated. With patience and knowledge it can be done easily enough at home, though some special tools are required. Two-stroke engines are particularly sensitive. Incorrect ignition timing may not be noticeable in the way the engine is behaving – until it comes to a dead stop with a hole burned in the piston. It pays to have the ignition of two-stroke engines adjusted professionally, and this includes the comparatively simple job of cleaning and adjusting the contact points.

Spark plugs deteriorate with use. The horn-like electrodes become pitted and wear out. They should be cleaned every 2–3,000 miles (refer to the handbook) and replaced every 5,000 miles. The condition of the spark plug often points to other engine troubles such as bad ignition timing.

The easiest way to test whether the ignition system is working is to remove the spark plug, lay it on the side of the cylinder block, and turn the engine over. You should be able to see the spark jumping, and hear it too. When replacing the spark plug, screw it in with the fingers for the first few turns to ensure it is not cross-threaded, and do not over-tighten it.

4 Piston

The piston is the engine's primary muscle. It is a precision-engineered plug of metal that slides up and down in a metal tube, or cylinder, in which it makes a very tight fit. The piston is connected to a crank, so that, when the piston goes up and down, the crank goes round and round.

In the simplest kinds of engine the spark plug is screwed into the top of the cylinder and there are two holes (ports) in the side of the cylinder which are sealed by the piston as it rises. These are for drawing in the petrol/air mixture and letting the burnt gases escape.

The heat of the explosions inside the cylinder reaches temperatures of about 700° F, so the outer surfaces of the cylinder block and the cylinder head are finned to disperse the heat into the slipstream.

The crank which the piston turns is called the crankshaft and is mounted in the lower part of the engine, called the crankcase. One end of the crankshaft drives the magneto, and the other end (by gear wheels through the gearbox and clutch) drives the rear wheel.

As you kick down on the starter lever, the crankshaft turns. The piston moves upwards, compressing the mixture of petrol/air against the top of the cylinder. The greater this compression the more powerful the engine is for its size and the greater the strain on it.

Just as the compression is at its greatest and the piston reaches its top position, the turning of the magneto on the end of the crankshaft produces the electric current that provides the spark.

The effect of the resulting explosion is an instantaneous expansion of the gases inside the cylinder. The piston is forced downwards with great force, giving power to the crankshaft which in turn drives the wheels.

The driving force of the engine is a series of very rapid explosions, each one ramming the piston downwards as soon as it reaches the top of its stroke. But after each explosion the spent gases have to escape to allow a fresh mixture of petrol/air to spurt in. This is done in one of two ways.

The simplest and cheapest engine, which is fitted to mopeds and most small motorcycles, is the two-stroke. This completes a full cycle in just two strokes of the piston – one up and one down. There is a power stroke for every revolution of the crankshaft.

The two-stroke engine has few moving parts, so it is simple and cheap and has good acceleration. But it is partly inefficient because it is never quite possible to get rid of all the exhaust gases, and therefore it uses more fuel and at tick-over runs roughly with a distinctive spluttery sound.

The four-stroke engine is more common in larger machines and

The two-stroke cycle

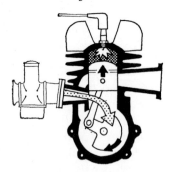 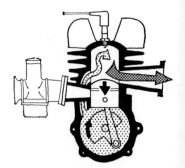

1 The piston moves up:
- compresses mixture where it is ignited by the spark
- allows mixture into crankcase

2 The piston moves down:
- allows exhaust gases out after the spark has ignited the mixture
- pushes mixture into cylinder

is almost universal in cars. It runs in a more measured way because the piston makes a power stroke only with every alternate revolution of the crankshaft, but requires more servicing.

Each of the piston's four strokes in every cycle has a different function: *Down* as the mixture explodes (the power stroke). *Up* to force out exhaust gases. *Down* to suck in more petrol/air. *Up* to compress it ready for the spark.

While the two-stroke engine can let the gases in and out of the cylinder through openings, the four-stroke engine must have a complicated system of valves which open and shut in sequence. These are operated by a revolving camshaft, which in turn is driven by a chain from the crankshaft.

When an engine has more than one cylinder, they can be placed

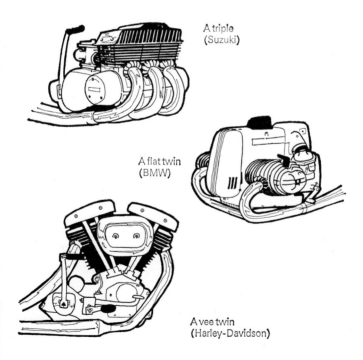

A triple
(Suzuki)

A flat twin
(BMW)

A vee twin
(Harley-Davidson)

side by side, in line, in a V (like some car engines), or be horizontally opposed. Each cylinder has its own spark plug and piston. The cylinders are timed to fire in sequence, so the power stroke of one piston is the induction stroke of another.

To make a tight seal between the piston and the cylinder wall (so that gases cannot escape downwards) and also to permit expansion due to heat, the barrel of the piston is fitted with two or three springy steel rings. These rub against the cylinder wall and the friction would soon make them red hot, with the metal melting and the engine parts fusing together, were it not for one vital ingredient – oil.

Oil lubricates all the moving parts, forming a thin and slippery buffer zone between the metal surfaces. This eliminates friction and absorbs some of the heat. If the oil is not clean, has been in use for too long, or is not of the right grade for the job, serious engine damage can result.

In two-stroke engines the oil is mixed with the petrol and introduced to the cylinder by way of the carburettor. In the cylinder the petrol evaporates, leaving the oil, which is sprayed over the moving parts.

Some two-stroke engines have separate oil tanks which must be refilled when buying petrol. Oil is fed into the carburettor by a pump which is operated by a second cable from the twistgrip.

The more conventional system is to mix the oil with the petrol at the same time as the tank is being filled. It is important to use exactly the recommended proportion of oil: too much oil causes engine overheating and too little does not do its lubricating job.

Four-stroke engines have a separate oil supply, sometimes in the bottom of the crank-case (wet sump) or in a separate tank (dry sump). The oil is splashed over the moving parts with every turn of the crankshaft, and a pump supplies oil to the camshaft and valve gear on top of the engine, from where it drains down again into the sump. The sump usually contains a filter which keeps the oil clean, but at predetermined intervals (refer to your handbook) the oil must be completely changed.

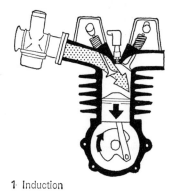

1 Induction

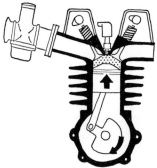

2 Compression

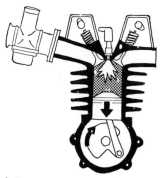

3 Power

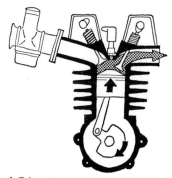

4 Exhaust

The four-stroke cycle

5 Transmission

As the explosion occurs in the cylinder, the piston goes down and the crankshaft spins. The next problem is to transmit this driving power from the crankshaft to the rear wheel, and to control it in different driving conditions.

The link between the engine and the rear wheel is called the transmission. In principle it is the same as that of a bicycle. The connection is made by a strong chain fitted to sprockets. The engine turns the chain which turns the wheel. But a motorcycle has two essential refinements – the clutch and the gearbox.

Clutch The clutch is designed to separate the engine from the transmission (gearbox and drive-chain) so that one can turn without affecting the other. When the clutch is disengaged (by operating the clutch lever on the left handlebar), the engine can run at any speed without turning the wheels.

Without a clutch the motorcycle would begin to move as soon as the engine started, and every time you had to stop on the road the engine would also stop.

The clutch helps the rider to feed engine power to the wheel by degrees. If the connection is made abruptly, the drag of the wheel makes the engine stop, or the rear wheel spins too fast and the bike goes out of control.

By releasing the clutch lever slowly, so that power reaches the wheel gradually, the machine moves away from a standing start with an easy gliding motion.

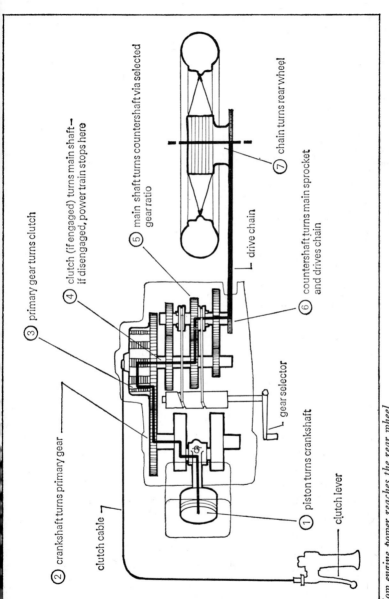

③ primary gear turns clutch

④ clutch (if engaged) turns main shaft — if disengaged, power train stops here

⑤ main shaft turns countershaft via selected gear ratio

⑦ chain turns rear wheel

drive chain

⑥ countershaft turns main sprocket and drives chain

② crankshaft turns primary gear

crankshaft turns primary gear

clutch cable

gear selector

① piston turns crankshaft

clutch lever

How engine power reaches the rear wheel

The common type of motorcycle clutch comprises a series of circular discs. These are fixed alternately to separate shafts. One shaft is turned by the engine, the other leads to the gearbox and the rear wheel. Some of the discs are metal, and some are lined with friction material like that of brake linings.

When the clutch is disengaged (the clutch lever on the handlebars is pulled inwards), the discs are separated and only those connected to the engine shaft spin round. As the clutch lever is released, the revolving discs begin to rub against the stationary ones and slowly make them turn. When the lever is fully released, and the clutch is engaged, all the discs turn together as one, forming a solid link between the engine and the gearbox.

On small motorcycles and mopeds some clutches are automatic. When the engine is idling, the clutch is disengaged. As revolutions are increased by operating the throttle, and the driveshaft turns faster and faster, weights in the clutch unit are forced outwards by centrifugal force. These press against a disc or metal drum which begins to turn and drives the wheels.

Gearbox   The effect of the gears of a motorcycle is the same as that of the gears of a bicycle. When a lot of push is required, as when starting off or going up a hill, a low gear is selected. This means the engine goes faster (or you have to pedal faster) and the rear wheel turns more slowly, but it has more power.

As speed is increased on the flat, the engine does not have to push so hard and a higher gear can be selected. By feeding the power through differently sized cog-wheels (called gears), the speed of the engine can always be matched to the speed of the wheels so that the two operate in harmony.

Simple motorcycles usually have three gears, but some more refined models have as many as six, which helps the rider to get the very best performance out of his engine.

Gears are changed by operating a lever with the foot. First, the clutch is disengaged to separate the engine from the wheels so that its speed can be adjusted to suit the new gear. Then the required

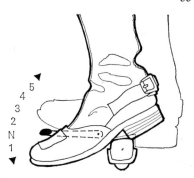

Lift the selector lever to change into higher gear, depress to change into lower gear. The selector lever works on a ratchet system so that a new gear is engaged each time it is depressed (or lifted) and released again

Selecting a gear

gear is selected by moving the lever up or down. Finally, the clutch is engaged again to reconnect the engine with the wheels.

Changing down to a lower gear must be done briskly, so that the machine does not lose too much speed. But changing up into a higher gear should be done in a leisured way.

The gear lever also has a neutral position, which means that no gear is engaged. This has the same effect as the clutch. It separates the engine from the wheels.

The gearbox is filled with oil which must be topped up and changed at intervals (refer to your handbook). On some models the clutch and the primary drive chain (which connects the clutch to the gearbox) are also submerged in oil to ensure smooth running.

Chain The main drive chain between the gearbox and the rear wheel must be carefully maintained because it deteriorates with use, wears out the sprockets, and collects dust which sticks to the oil and grease. Some models have a protective guard that encloses the chain.

A loose chain imposes strain on the engine and if it breaks it can cause an accident. To adjust the tension of the chain the rear wheel must be moved backwards, but, if the position of the rear wheel is altered, ensure that it is always square-on. If the wheel is out of alignment, the machine will handle dangerously and could go out of control on a bend.

Some machines have endless chains which cannot be split for easy removal, but most have a special link which can be undone by removing a clip. When refitting the clip, make sure that the open end always faces away from the direction of travel or it may work loose. You can test the condition of a chain by laying it out in a straight line and measuring the amount of stretch; if it is more than a quarter of an inch per foot, the chain is worn out and should be replaced.

6   Support systems

Running in ideal conditions on a test bench, an engine gives no trouble for thousands of hours. Fitting it into the frame of a motor-cycle, and expecting it to do its job in wind and rain, heat and dust, is a different story.

Petrol must be delivered to the carburettor when the machine is banked on a corner, or leaping through the air. The spark must reach the plug in lashing rain, when a speck of water in the wrong place could cause a short circuit.

Also this entire package of machinery is put together in such a way that a rider can make it turn, slow down, speed up, or stop suddenly. While performing these actions, on rough roads or smooth, the whole thing must be in balance so that it does not topple over on a corner or wobble when the brakes go on.

For control, balance, and the quality known as 'handleability' the engine depends on a number of support systems – electrics, brakes, steering, suspension, and grip on the road.

Handleability is the way a machine feels while it is being ridden. At all times it should feel in balance. The rider must feel nothing but confidence in its ability to carry out his orders. How it does this is the art of motorcycle design.

Motorcycle and rider should blend together in the kind of total harmony you share with a pair of comfortable shoes. It is not the kind of harmony that exists between horse and rider: if a motorcycle has a will of its own, something is wrong.

The engine might be the heart of the motorcycle, the ignition its nervous system, the control cables its tendons, and the wheels its legs. But its brains and its will-power should be found only in the driver's own head.

It is important to think of a motorcycle as a number of different systems, all working together but each one totally dependent on the others. If one fails, they all fail. The rider is another system – the eyes, ears, and brains of the outfit. If one of the mechanical systems fails, the rider too is brought down.

Many riders lavish a great deal of attention and care on the engine but overlook the other systems on which it depends. The best engine in the world is useless if the motorcycle's tyre pressures are not adjusted correctly, or the control cables are stiff for want of a drop of oil.

For safety it is these secondary systems that are the most import-ant. The engine makes the machine go. But the rider should be more concerned about what makes it stop, and what keeps it on the road.

7 Brakes

Safety depends on good brakes, not on engine performance. A motorcycle should never be ridden unless its brakes are in tip-top condition.

Brakes work by friction. This is reduced if the brakes get wet, or hot. In rain you should always drive more slowly, partly because the road may be slippery but also because the brakes may not work

The braking system on a typical motorcycle

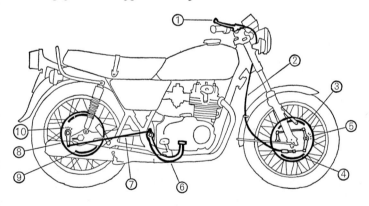

1	Front brake lever	6	Rear brake pedal
2	Front brake cable	7	Rear brake rod
3	Front brake drum	8	Rear brake drum
4	Brake shoe	9	Brake shoe
5	Wear indicator	10	Wear indicator

as well as usual. After driving through a ford it is essential to dry them out by driving for a short distance with the brakes on.

Prolonged use, as when travelling down a long hill with the brakes on, can cause them to fade. In other words they work less and less well as they get hot. You should brake in short and firm bursts then release, giving them a few moments to cool down.

There are two types of brake common on motorcycles:

Drum brakes These are fitted to most small machines and are usually found on the rear wheels of larger machines. There are two curved metal arms called shoes fitted inside a drum. The drum is attached to the wheel and goes round with it. On each shoe is riveted a layer of special friction material called the lining.

When the brake is operated by lever or pedal, the two shoes are made to move outwards so that they rub hard against the spinning drum and slow it down. With use the linings wear out, so they have to be adjusted and after a few thousand miles need to be replaced.

Adjustment is a simple matter of tightening the nut at the end of the control cable (refer to your handbook) until you feel the brake dragging when you spin the wheel. Then release the nut until the wheel spins easily. Most machines have wear indicators which

A drum brake

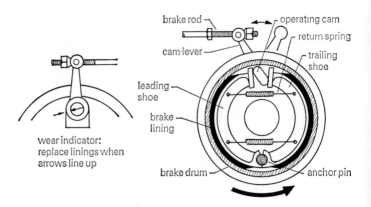

brake rod
operating cam
cam·lever
return spring
trailing shoe
leading shoe
brake lining
brake drum
anchor pin
wear indicator: replace linings when arrows line up

show when the adjustment is fully taken up and the linings need replacement.

Hydraulic disc brakes   These are very powerful brakes usually fitted only to the front wheel of big and powerful machines. A steel disc fitted to the front wheel revolves between two pads of friction material. When the brake lever is operated the pads are squeezed tightly together, trapping the disc and slowing the wheel. The pads are self-adjusting and on most machines there is a red line which shows when they need replacement.

Instead of a cable connecting the brake lever and the brake unit there is a tube of special fluid. When the lever is operated, it works a piston which pushes this hydraulic fluid against another piston at the other end. The second piston operates the brake.

Hydraulic brakes are firmer and provide more power, but the fluid must be kept in good condition. A reserve of fluid is kept in the master cylinder, which is usually mounted on the handlebars and is transparent, so keeping a check on the level of fluid is easy. If the level drops, a leak has occurred and the system requires *immediate* attention. At certain intervals (refer to your handbook) the system must be drained and new fluid provided.

A disc brake

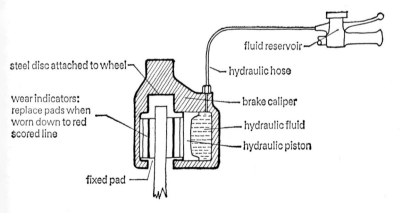

fluid reservoir

steel disc attached to wheel

hydraulic hose

wear indicators: replace pads when worn down to red scored line

brake caliper

hydraulic fluid

hydraulic piston

fixed pad

Use only the type of hydraulic brake fluid recommended in the handbook and never be tempted to use some other kind of fluid such as oil. Air bubbles in the fluid may cause brake failure, so never shake the container before topping up the master cylinder. Brake fluid can damage paint and plastic. Do not use old fluid which absorbs moisture from the air and can boil in the brake cylinders when the brakes are applied.

8 Electrics

The simplest kinds of moped and motorcycle do not have batteries. Power for the horn and lights comes direct from the magneto, as does the supply for the ignition. The disadvantage is that when the engine is ticking over slowly, as when waiting at traffic lights, the magneto is also turning slowly and not making much electricity. The result is that the lights go dim.

This can be overcome by fitting a very small battery which does not add too much weight to a small machine. It is recharged by magneto and supplies power to the tail light and horn so that they always work properly for safety. The headlight is powered direct from the magneto.

Larger machines can have bigger batteries that are able to do more work. Some have an alternator or a dynamo in place of the magneto. These are more reliable, work better at low revs, and provide a more powerful current.

The battery stores electricity. Like a water tank in the attic of a house it supplies all the different needs and itself is constantly recharged. The level of acid in each cell of the battery drops with use and has to be regularly topped up with distilled water (refer to your handbook).

An electric starter uses a great deal of power and it takes quite a few miles of running to replace the current it has used. Therefore, if a machine is used only for short trips, the drain on the battery gets steadily worse until it goes flat.

Wires carry the electrical current from the positive terminal of

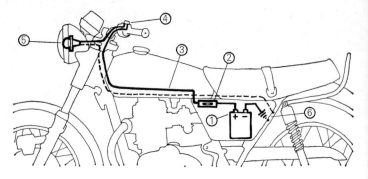

1 Electricity comes from the positive terminal of the battery
2 Passes through the fuse
3 Travels along wire taped to the frame
4 Passes through the switch on the handlebar
5 Illuminates the light bulb
6 Returns through the frame of the machine to the earthing strap connected to the
   negative terminal of the battery, so completing a round trip *(circuit)*

How electricity reaches the lights

the battery through switches on the handlebars to the different lights, indicators, and horn. The wires are usually different colours, so you can refer to the wiring diagram in the handbook and find out which wire does which job.

Before it can flow an electrical current must make a circuit, or loop. The current flows from the positive terminal of the battery (marked +), along the wire, through the switch, which must be in the 'on' position, through the light bulb or horn mechanism, and back to the negative (marked −) battery terminal. Or it can flow in reverse, from negative to positive, depending on the design of the system (this is explained in your handbook).

The return journey is not made along a wire but through the steel frame of the motorcycle itself. This is called the 'earth' because it provides a common link between the battery and all the electrical parts. For it to function properly the negative terminal of every electrical fitting must be in firm contact.

A poor earth contact is often the explanation for a fault such as a flickering light bulb. The wire and switch and bulb might be in perfect order, but if there is a speck of rust at the point where the bulb makes contact with the socket (which is in direct contact with the frame) the current may not be able to get through.

Another common fault is the earth strap between the frame of the machine and the negative terminal of the battery. If this breaks or becomes dislodged, or if the terminal is not clean and in good condition, all the electrics are affected.

Small motorcycles generally have a six-volt system but larger ones, like cars, have a twelve-volt system. Replacement bulbs and other electrical fittings are not interchangeable and it is important to fit only the right spares for the job.

In most systems a fuse (sometimes more than one) is incorporated as a safety measure. This is a piece of thin wire in a glass tube. It is strong enough to take a certain amount of current. If too much current flows through, it melts and interrupts the circuit, preventing damage or even fire. Always carry two or three spare fuses of the required grade (refer to your handbook). One might 'blow' through vibration. If a second also goes, it indicates an electrical fault which must be rectified.

9 Suspension and steering

The suspension system has two important functions. One is to absorb bumps, giving the rider a soft and comfortable ride and preventing the machine from shaking itself to bits. The other is to ensure that the wheels remain in contact with the ground. A sure sign of a suspension system not doing its job is the wheels bouncing or hopping on the road surface so that the machine is difficult to control. The springiness that absorbs the bumps must be controlled. If the rebound were not dampened, the springs would have a catapult effect and the machine would travel along as if it were a pogo stick.

A complete shock absorber consists of a spring and a damper.

The dampers are metal tubes which slide one inside the other like a telescope. The telescope can be shut quickly, but it cannot be opened quickly because oil flowing through a small valve between the two cylinders has a friction effect.

On the rear of the machine the damper usually fits inside the spring. On the front the spring is inside the damper, which is part of the front-fork assembly. At intervals the oil in the dampers must be changed (refer to your handbook).

You can test the suspension system by leaning heavily on the front or rear end of the machine then releasing it. The machine should not leap upwards as if spring-loaded, but rise slowly and evenly. This shows that the dampers are doing their job.

Some small and cheap mopeds do not have a suspension system and rely only on the tyres, like a bicycle. These are capable only of

10 Wheels and tyres

The tyres of a motorcycle are its only contact with the ground. If the tyres lose their grip, the machine goes out of control. Yet the total amount of rubber in contact with the road at any one time, and supporting the entire dynamic stress of bike and rider hurtling round a bend at speed, is no greater than the soles of a tightrope-walker's slippers.

The tread of the tyre is scientifically designed to provide maximum grip. It is channelled to push water aside on wet roads. If road water is as thick as a penny, a tyre travelling at 60 mph must move about 100 gallons of water a minute. If the tread is not deep enough to pump this water away, the tyre rises up on its own bow-wave so that it glides over the water and has no contact with the road. This is called aquaplaning, and it is the nearest thing to flying without wings. When it happens bike and rider are on the brink of disaster.

The air inside the front and rear tyres weighs a little more than one ounce but it is the most important weight on the machine. The amount of air pumped into the tyre must be exactly as recommended in the handbook, and kept that way.

If the pressure is too high, the tyres will be too hard and the machine will bounce and skip over the road; braking will be poor and the centre part of the tyre will quickly wear thin.

A low pressure makes the tyre floppy; the machine feels unstable on corners and will wobble; the edges of the tyre will rapidly wear out.

Tyre pressures must be checked regularly and frequently: once a day is not too often, once a week is not often enough. They might be correct time after time, but the one time you don't check them might be the time you need them most. Pressures should be checked when the tyres are cold. The pressure gauges on many garage forecourts are inaccurate, so it pays to carry your own gauge, which costs only a few pence and is no larger than a pen.

The tyre should be suitable for the use to which it is being put. On public roads this is a matter of law as well as safety. A knobbly cross-country tyre can be dangerous on smooth roads because only a small part of it is in contact with the road. This means that there is not enough rubber to provide grip when cornering or braking, and the tyre will wear out quickly.

Also the depth of tread on the tyre must be at least 1 mm all the way round and for three quarters of the width. Except in the case of small moped tyres built for slow speeds (which legally must have a tread pattern that is 'clearly visible'), this is too low for safety. A motorcycle with only 1 mm of tread on its tyres is a death-trap. It is the centre of the tyre that is important. The tread at the centre should be no less than 2 mm in depth.

Different tyres for different jobs

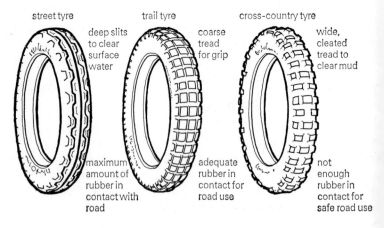

| street tyre | trail tyre | cross-country tyre |

deep slits to clear surface water

maximum amount of rubber in contact with road

coarse tread for grip

adequate rubber in contact for road use

wide, cleated tread to clear mud

not enough rubber in contact for safe road use

Motorcycle tyres have inner tubes (unlike car tyres which are mostly tubeless). The tube must be kept in tip-top condition. Do not struggle along with a patched tube but use a new one, because a blow-out on a motorcycle is no joke. Also make regular weekly inspections of the tyres for sidewall damage, flints, and bulges. The British Standards Institution warns against using aerosol-type puncture repair outfits.

The sizes of tyre are described in a certain way. A typical small motorcycle tyre is a 2·50–17–4PR.

2·50   This is the width of the tread in inches (2½ inches); sometimes it is measured in millimetres.

17   This is the diameter of the wheel-rim in inches.

4PR   This is the ply-rating, indicating that the tyre is made of four layers; stronger tyres have six layers.

High-powered motorcycles capable of more than 95 mph are fitted with special high-speed tyres which are graded according to their top-speed capability. For wheels of more than thirteen inches diameter the markings are:

No mark   Tyre can be used up to 95 mph.

S   Tyre can be used up to 110 mph.

H   Tyre can be used up to 125 mph.

V   Tyre can be used at speeds higher than 125 mph.

This mark would be included with the tyre measurement, for example: 3·25H19–4PR. Do not use a radial tyre on a motorcycle. This type of tyre is common on cars but is not suitable for two-wheelers. It is marked with an R, which comes after the speed rating (for example 6·50SR14–6PR).

Setting up a wheel so that it is perfectly round and balanced is a skilful job and requires special workshop equipment: even motorcycle workshops often send wheels away to be done by specialists.

Using string to align the wheels

The spokes should be checked regularly by spinning the wheel and tapping each one lightly with a screw-driver; a loose spoke has a tinny sound. Tighten one or two, but, if more than two need adjustment, the roundness of the wheel might be distorted. If a spoke is tightened by more than one turn, its outer end could spike the inner tube.

The position of the rear wheel is adjustable to allow the right tension to be set on the drive chain. This means it can be put out of alignment unless you take care to check it from time to time.

If the wheel is out of alignment, the machine will corner superbly one way, but wobble and prove very hard to control the other way. It will also scuff the tread and wear out the tyre.

Most machines have marks which assist in setting the wheel true. You can check it against a plank (with a notch cut out of it to go round the stand) but this method is not ideal because most machines have a wider wheel on the rear. It is best done with a piece of string tied to a spoke at the rear of the rear wheel and laid first along one side of the machine and then along the other.

11 Do-it-yourself workshop

A typical small motorcycle is a simple piece of machinery. It is easy to understand and easy to work on. Routine maintenance and simple repairs can be done at home using nothing but the machine's own tool-kit. You don't need much mechanical aptitude beyond patience and thoroughness.

On the other hand, if you do a job at all, it must be done carefully and it must be done well. You can't take chances with a motorcycle. It is not a toy. If adjustments to such things as the brakes, chain tension, and lights are not done properly, it can be a death-trap.

While the machine is still new it is a good idea to spend an hour or two inspecting the engine so that you know what certain parts look like when they are in good condition. If you look at the spark plug while it is new, you can tell later on if the electrodes appear unduly pitted or oiled up. Look at the way the points open and shut (don't try to adjust them) so that you will be able to tell later on when they should be replaced.

The secret of good motorcycle maintenance is to make routine checks, looking for trouble before it occurs. Being open to the elements, a motorcycle is susceptible to damp, dirt, salt, and vibration. At least once a week you should look for signs of wear and tear, such as chafe on a cable, or an oil leak, which could spell trouble later.

The most important nut on a motorcycle is the one that is loose. It takes only a couple of minutes to go round the bike with spanners and a screwdriver checking all the nuts, bolts, and screws and at the same time having a close look at everything.

Hand-washing detergent (available in accessory shops) is ideal for cleaning difficult corners of the engine. Brush it on with a bristly dish-washing brush then hose it off with a gentle pressure. Alternatively use a rag soaked in petrol or paraffin.

To do any serious repair work on the engine, which entails dismantling some of it, a set of good-quality tools will be required. Different types of thread – metric (continental), BSF/BSW (British, now obsolete), or unified (American) – require different spanners because the bolt-heads differ, so, if you are buying new tools, first find out what system is used on your machine. Most machines are now metric.

It is important to use tools that fit. Wrong sizes do damage. Do not use undue force, do not hit things with a metal hammer, and do not hit threads or thread-ends. Before starting, it is essential to get hold of a workshop manual (usually available from a library) which explains your machine in detail and shows in pictures how it comes apart and fits together again.

For taking the engine apart completely a lot of special tools are required. Without them the job can be difficult and your efforts might do damage.

The most important thing in home mechanics is to know how good you are – and to know when to stop. Any amateur can do simple jobs like oiling and adjusting the cables, adjusting the headlight, and topping up the battery. These jobs are essential and can be done after referring to the handbook.

It takes a little more of an expert to diagnose a fault in the ignition, to clean the petrol filters, remove the rear wheel, adjust the carburettor, or change the oil.

Most people with an interest in mechanics and a reasonable set of tools should be able to do jobs like relining the brakes, cleaning the carburettor, cleaning and readjusting the spark plug, and removing the cylinder head.

If you are doubtful about your ability, do not tackle any job that might affect the safety or balance of the machine. Take it to a workshop and have it done by professionals. If you notice any form of instability while riding, first check tyre pressure, then check rear wheel alignment (see page 150). It is not advisable to do anything else except take it to a workshop.

Two-stroke engines are simpler than four-stroke engines in every respect except the ignition timing, which ought to be checked in a workshop unless you have special equipment and a certain amount of experience.

On every machine certain routine servicing jobs have to be done at regular intervals. These are listed in the handbook. One group of jobs has to be done every 2,000 miles (or every two months) and another group every 4,000 miles (or every four months).

Most of these routine servicing jobs can be done at home with a good set of tools and the help of the handbook and a workshop manual. They are not listed here because they vary widely for different models.

Routine servicing is critically important. Follow the instructions in the handbook. If you do not do it yourself, be sure to have it done in a workshop. When servicing is missed out, or skimped, the engine runs badly, wears out more quickly, and costs more to run. If such things as the brakes are not serviced regularly – well, one day you might not be able to stop when you need to.

After a routine service the machine may not appear noticeably different. You might think you have done all that work, or spent all that money, for nothing. The difference, however, is that now you know it is *right*.

This gives you confidence in the machine, confidence which helps to make you into a better rider.

Daily checks   These checks take only a minute or so to complete but they are critical to your safety and to trouble-free riding:

1 Is there petrol in the tank?

2 Tyre pressures (look for damage at the same time); check while tyres are cold.

3 Are lights (including brake light) and horn working?

4 If the engine is a two-stroke, is oil visible in the oil tank?

As you drive off:
5 Check front and rear brakes separately.

First time you stop:
6 If the engine is a four-stroke, check oil level while the machine is hot, level, and stopped.

Weekly checks   This may seem a long list, but a comprehensive inspection of the machine once a week is essential. The whole job takes less than five minutes. It is mainly a visual examination, which can be done as you clean the bike. Anything that is not quite right should be adjusted on the spot and it may not need attention for several more weeks, but at least you have the satisfaction of always knowing that it is right.

1 Spin wheels to check that brakes are not binding.

2 Adjust front and rear brakes.*

3 Check clutch adjustment.*

4 Check throttle control adjustment.*

5 Check engine idling speed and adjust.*

6 Check that controls are operating smoothly; if not, lubricate the cables.

7 Check that steering movement is not trapping any cables or wires, and that none are fraying.

8 Remove flints from tyres and inspect for damage.

9 Apply front brake and rock machine forwards to check for movement in the steering head and front forks.

10 Rock wheels sideways to check bearings.

11 Spin wheels and tap spokes, listening for a dull sound that indicates a loose spoke.

12 Check battery level and top up with distilled water if necessary.

13 Check electrical connections to ensure none are corroding or have shaken loose.

14 Check tightness of screws, nuts, and bolts.

15 Check chain tension.*

16 Look for leaking petrol and oil.

17 If brakes are hydraulic, check level of hydraulic fluid and inspect pipe for leaks.

18 Check rear-wheel alignment.

19 Check level of gearbox oil.*

20 Check with handbook for any other jobs to be done.

* These jobs are usually detailed in the owner's handbook.

IV Sport on two wheels

1 Motorcycle competition

The cost of participating in motorcycle sport can be as little as a tank of petrol. Or it can run to thousands of pounds.

You can compete in an official event from the age of six; and carry on until you are too old to kick the starter.

Some events require nerve, skill, and courage of the highest order – such as Grand Prix racing in which racers reach speeds of more than 170 mph and enormous fortunes are to be made.

In other events balance and control are what count, and there are times when a speed of just half a mile an hour is a little too fast for comfort.

Brute force and horsepower are what win some events, and the machine needs special preparation and has to be taken to the track on a trailer.

But there are many other competitions to which you can ride, and even take part with a friend sitting on the pillion. With an ordinary machine you can take part in club rallies, and a *concours d'élégance*, which is a kind of motorcycle beauty contest.

A trail bike allows you to tour on roads and take to rough tracks and byways through the countryside where there is official right-of-way for vehicles but not much of a surface.

In some branches of the sport the death and accident rate is frightening, but in others the sport has a nearly perfect record. This means you can choose your own level of risk – only some motorcycle sport is dangerous.

From schoolboys to veterans, the number of riders who take part in competitions on two-wheelers is very great indeed. The Auto-Cycle Union, which comes under the wing of the Royal Automobile Club, is the governing body and controller of motorcycle sport in England and Wales. The Scottish ACU looks after about forty clubs in Scotland. Competition in both Eire and Northern Ireland is run by the Motor Cycle Union of Ireland (addresses on page 173).

More than 600 clubs with a membership of 50,000 are affiliated to the ACU. Every year the ACU issues 18,000 competition licences. All over the country scores of events, big and small, take place every weekend.

There is also a large youth division in the ACU which runs scrambling and grass-track competitions for riders aged between six and sixteen. Schoolboy clubs are found in all parts of the country and hold events nearly every weekend between spring and autumn.

All motorcycling competition is strictly organized and run under close rules. Competitors must have an ACU competition licence, which costs a couple of pounds a year depending on the type. For speed events the licence requires a medical certificate.

Also machines must be correctly prepared in accordance with strict rules to ensure that other competitors cannot be injured. Every rider must be properly togged up and wear a crash helmet approved by the ACU (this is additional to the kitemark of the British Standards Institution).

The ACU Handbook, which is issued annually, lists the names and addresses of the secretaries of all affiliated clubs. In England and Wales the clubs are grouped in nineteen areas, called centres. Scotland is another centre. A member of a particular club can compete in any event organized by a club of the same centre. There are also inter-centre competitions, national events, and international events.

If you want to join a club, write in the first place to the ACU, who will put you in touch with the secretary of your local centre. From the secretary you can find out which club in your area best suits the kind of competitions you want to enter.

If you are not able to afford a motorcycle, you can still have a lot of fun by joining a club and volunteering to help at meetings as a track marshal, pit steward, or parking attendant. This is the quickest way to make friends in the sport, because every club is short of helpers.

Later, when you buy your own machine (perhaps cheaply, from another member), you will already have learned a lot about the sport and you will have made friends who will be able to help and give advice.

Besides local clubs which run their own events there are also national clubs which have a particular common interest, such as owners of Triumph machines, or vintage motorcycles, or those interested in drag racing.

Motorcycle sport is reputable, friendly, and need not be expensive. It provides recreation, pleasure, and excitement for thousands of people. But it can be given a bad name by riders who 'practise' by racing up and down streets or scrambling on heaths and open country where other people expect to find peace and quiet.

It is much better to join a club and take advantage of its practice sessions which take place where nobody will be offended, than to make trouble for yourself – and all other motorcyclists – by inconsiderate riding.

2 Scrambling (motocross)

Racing cross-country is rough, tough, not fast enough to be dangerous but quite fast enough to be thrilling, and wonderful fun. The sport is called scrambling, and is internationally known as 'motocross'. It takes nerve, control, balance, great determination, and (as far as the bike is concerned) punchy acceleration in the lower speed ranges.

Riders are togged up with colourful plastic armour, strong leather boots, a body belt to protect the stomach, and a face mask for protection against flying mud and stones. The less skin showing the better.

Average speed of a race is about 30 mph, ranging from plugging through mud in low gear to blasting along undulating turf at full revs (which is like trying to take off with no wings). There are spills in plenty but the ground is soft.

About 4,000 boys aged between six and sixteen (inclusive) take part in schoolboy scrambling events. These are valuable nurseries for adult competition. The meetings have an excellent safety record – an occasional broken leg but nothing more serious. Machines for schoolboy events are made for the job and can be bought off the showroom floor with no special conversion needed. The total cost of entering the sport with new machine and equipment (at 1976 prices) is about £1,000.

Scrambling originated in Britain during the 1920s and since the Second World War has become popular in Europe and America. Events are held on circuits about a mile long with as many natural obstacles as possible – puddles, bumps, ditches, jumps, ruts, and steep slopes.

The secret of winning races is to play the throttle as delicately as a violin, feeding power through to the rear wheel so it does not spin. The rider's foot should touch the ground as seldom as possible.

During the scrambling season from early spring to late autumn scores of club and open events are held, mainly in the southern half of England. Most races are over-subscribed because the sport is so popular. To give good riders a fair chance there is a grading system which awards points for wins. When a rider is graded 'expert', it is easier for him to take part in a race. For 'juniors' it is a matter of being first in with an entry form.

In ordinary scrambling (i.e. not for boys) there are two main classes of machine, up to 250cc and up to 500cc. In schoolboy scrambling there is a general limit of 125cc, with lower limits for younger age groups. A schoolboy scrambling machine must have knobbly tyres, balls on the ends of the control levers, folding foot-rests, silencer, chainguards, mudguards, and a cut-out button so that the engine can be stopped if the rider falls off.

3 Grass-track and sand racing

This is a fast and gruelling form of motorcycle racing that is some-where between scrambling and speedway. Like scrambling there are a number of youth division clubs that promote races.

A speedway-shaped course is laid out in a smooth field or on hard sand. Races are usually short but fast. Scrambling-type machines can be entered but are not really competitive against properly prepared dirt-track racers, which are designed for fierce acceleration and power-sliding round bends.

Speedway-type machines have tiny fuel tanks that carry just enough petrol for one race of three or four laps. Top grass-track riders go on to make their names (and fortunes) in speedway racing.

This is a violent and often dangerous sport that draws huge crowds. Most riders are professionals. On a tight track of cinders or shale, only a quarter of a mile per lap, the racers reach 90 mph on the straights and 60 mph on the bends.

4   Road racing

This is the glamour sport of motorcycling – where fortunes are made and the most serious casualties occur. A top rider requires nerve, skill, and courage of the highest order.

Look at the story of champion Barry Sheene. He became a world-class rider by the age of twenty-four, earning more than £2,000 a week and racing in events all over the world.

While practising for the biggest race of 1975 at Daytona in America he crashed at the terrifying speed of 175 mph – and survived. Not only that, within ten weeks he was back on his bike and racing again. This is the steel of which top riders are made.

In Britain road racing actually takes place off the road – on aerodrome circuits and race tracks such as Brands Hatch, Oulton Park, Mallory Park, and Silverstone.

Only at one place do motorcycles race on public roads, and that is the most gruelling, testing, dangerous, and thrilling motorcycle race in the world – the Isle of Man International Tourist Trophy.

This race held every June covers six laps of a circuit that twists for thirty-eight miles through two major towns, five villages, and the rugged Isle of Man countryside. From sea level it climbs 1,640 feet to Snaefell, twisting over bridges, winding through gullies, and even crossing railway lines.

The roads are made for cars and lorries, not for motorcycles *averaging* more than 100 mph around the course. There is every possible hazard. It is a road racer's dream, but a track official's nightmare. Since the race started in 1907 more than a hundred riders have been killed.

The event lasts a week, with another week of practice beforehand when the circuit is made available at dusk and at dawn. In the racing more than 500 riders take part, leaving in pairs every ten seconds. The race has the raw thrill of motor sport in its pioneer days.

To be successful at road racing requires absolute dedication and a pocket full of money. Many riders are financed by firms in exchange for advertising (this is called sponsorship). The motorcycle manufacturers such as Suzuki also have their own works teams for which they employ the world's best riders and invest large sums of money to boost the image of their products.

Without spending a fortune you can nevertheless have a lot of fun in the sport. Many clubs run track races for ordinary members who can ride their machines to the meeting, prepare them by taping over the glass lenses and removing the centre stands, then enter a race.

The main tracks like Silverstone and Brands Hatch have open practice sessions on certain days of the year. Any motorcycle rider can use the track for a small fee. Although there are strict track rules there are no speed limits.

5 Drag racing and sprinting

Drag racing is a rapidly growing spectator sport that involves both motorcycles and cars. The aim is to cover a distance of a quarter of a mile from a standing start in the quickest possible time.

Entries are grouped according to the type of machinery. In each group they leave in pairs, so it is a simple knock-out competition with the fastest going through to the next round.

At the top end of the scale are the fantastically expensive, supremely engineered dragsters that cover the distance in about eight seconds and reach speeds of about 150 mph.

The machines have two 1,500cc engines, both supercharged. There is a large rear wheel with a wide, flat tyre. The chassis is very long and the rider lies face down along it. There are no silencers, so the brutal roar of the engine makes the ground tremble.

Then, in a cloud of rubber-smoke and fumes, the rider lets out the clutch and the dragster goes away like a bullet.

At the bottom end of the scale are ordinary street machines with no mechanical modifications. Winning form on this type of motorcycle requires reliability and consistency rather than sheer speed.

A typical time for a 250cc street motorcycle for the quarter mile distance is 14·86 seconds, reaching a speed of 87 mph. If you already have a good street machine, this class of drag racing is probably the cheapest form of motor sport in which speed plays a part, and it puts you in the pits with the enormous drag-racing cars which burn nitro-methane or alcohol and do the quarter mile in an amazing six seconds, reaching speeds of more than 220 mph.

Sprinting is similar to drag racing but it is run against the clock and is not a race. The difference is that in sprinting the rider can move when he is ready, but in drag racing he must go when the starting light shows green.

Half the fun of sprinting and drag racing is building the machines, which are highly complicated and tuned to a fantastic pitch. Competitors have to be at least sixteen years old.

6 Trials riding

If scrambling is a kind of motorcycle steeplechase, then a motor-cycle trial is more of a point-to-point. It takes place on a long circular route using roads and cross-country sections. And it is real wilderness. The motorcycle is expected to be not so much a horse as a mountain goat.

Parts of the course may follow a stream, wind through woods, skirt the lip of a cliff, and even go over logs and boulders. These difficult sections are short, some only twenty or thirty yards long, but observers are placed to watch every move you make and deduct marks each time you put a foot on the ground.

Competitors can go as slowly as they like (only a few events are timed). The art is to finish the course with as few penalty points as possible. Trial riders are mostly amateurs and the sport is not dangerous.

Trial riding is a great test of skill and is not expensive. The machine can be small. It should be light, compact, and narrow, with good ground clearance and a very low gear so it can travel slower than walking pace yet have plenty of power.

On the difficult sections the observers deduct one mark for dabbing (a quick prod at the ground to maintain balance), three marks for footing (paddling with both feet), and five marks for stopping or falling off.

Trials are popular mainly in the north of England and most are held during the winter. About 1,600 trials are held every year, as well as international events.

Some trials go on for several days and are known as 'enduros'. The International Six Days Trial is held in a different country every year. It covers 150 miles cross-country every day and includes timed stages, hill-climbs, and observed sections. During the event only the tyres may be changed.

Trial riding can be practised at home in the backyard without the engine going. With the handlebars on full lock you should be able to stand on the outside foot-rest then – without touching the ground or moving the machine – change to opposite lock and climb across to the other foot-rest on the opposite side of the machine. Slow riding along planks and in figures-of-eight around obstacles placed a bike-length apart is also good practice.

7 Green-laning (trail riding)

This is not an organized sport, but often groups of motorcyclists do it together. It is a kind of cross-country route march. Riding trail-type machines (suitable for cross-country or road use) they look for long-distance tracks through the countryside.

Driving along cart tracks and leafy lanes fit for ramblers and horse riders is undoubtedly satisfying and pleasurable but it leads to a lot of trouble because ramblers and horse riders don't like encountering groups of motorcyclists with revving engines. Nor does the noise of motorcycles splashing through streams and roaring around sand-pits go well with bird-song and the peaceful buzz of insects on a summer's day.

Motorcycles do have legal access to routes marked on Ordnance

Survey maps as RUPP – road used as public path. For this kind of track the maps have a special symbol which can be found in the key.

Unfortunately resentment by countryside lovers is causing a lot of these routes to be re-designated to exclude motor vehicles. Many trail riders who know of good cross-country routes keep quiet about them because over-use might stir up local trouble.

Many motorcyclists unwittingly make the situation worse by riding around on public commons and in popular places such as the New Forest.

Trail riding can be fun, but you must be considerate. Do not travel up and down the same piece of track. Keep revs low and drive sensibly; don't turn your ride into a scramble. Ride only where there is a recognized trail and where you have legal right of way. Do not ride in large groups, but for your own safety (in case you have an accident) don't ride in remote areas alone.

Index